Timely Types

TIMELY TYPES

The Psychology of Personality: From Jung to Myers and Briggs

Hugh R. LeSure

edited by Shawn LeSure

A TETRAGRAM PRESS BOOK

Copyright © 2017 by Hugh R. LeSure

Published by Tetragram Press

ISBN 978-0999398906

Printed in the United States of America

To those for whom belief is not enough

"The difference between the 'natural' individuation process, which runs its course unconsciously, and the one that's consciously realized, is tremendous. In the first case, consciousness nowhere intervenes; the end remains as dark as the beginning. In the second case, so much darkness comes to light that the personality is permeated with light, and consciousness necessarily gains in scope and insight. The encounter between conscious and unconscious has to ensure that the light which shines in the darkness is not only comprehended by the darkness, but comprehends it."

—Jung

Table of Contents

It is Time for Timely Types

Inscribed on the Temple of Apollo at Delphi were the words "know thyself." These famous words have served as inspiration to generations of the world's greatest artists, thinkers and philosophers, including Socrates. In *Apology*, Plato informs the reader that, according to the oracle at Delphi, there was no one wiser than Socrates—an assertion Socrates did not boast about but put to the test. Socrates believed that by finding the wisest of his contemporaries and examining their insights, he would prove the oracle was wrong about him. He, therefore, sought out politicians, poets, and artisans, but his investigation only confirmed the oracle's statement:

> Although I do not suppose that [any] of us knows anything really beautiful and good, I am better off than [they are] - for [they] know nothing, yet think that [they] know. I neither know nor think that I know. In this latter particular, then, I seem to have slightly the advantage of [them]. . . . I was conscious that I knew nothing at all.[1]

It is natural to wonder how someone who claims to know nothing at all could come to know that the oracle was correct; and if one reads Plato's other dialogues, it becomes clear Socrates knows quite a lot and is respected for his knowledge. The illogic is palpable and must have been obvious to someone of Plato's intellect. Clearly, this "nothing" is actually something, but what could it be?

It would be well to consider art because in the great works, the whole of the human spirit shows its face. Beethoven's Ninth Symphony, with its triumphant "Ode to Joy" finale, has a sorrowful and dark beginning. Salvador Dali's *The Persistence of Memory* not only unites foreground and background, high and low, light and shadow, it also combines the familiar with the bizarre and, most famously, explores softness in contrast to hardness.

The same principle is at work in the sciences. Newton saw it when he wrote, "To every action, there is an equal and opposite reaction." Furthermore, there are positive and negative numbers, electrons and protons, motion and repose, macroscopic and microscopic, empirical and theoretical, depth and height. The principle is also operative in daily life, for there is no mountain without valley, no parent without child, no conservative without liberal.

Carl Jung saw this principle of opposites at work in the human mind. The pair of opposites with which Jung was most concerned was the conscious and unconscious minds, a pairing that results in further oppositions: introversion and extraversion, feeling and thought, sensing and intuition, rational and irrational, ego and shadow, objective and subjective. Central to his theory of types are these opposites, which Jung spent a significant part of his career not only exploring but working to reconcile. Jung's landmark book, *Psychological Types*, was first released in German in 1921 and in English in 1923. The book is brilliant, but not written for the common person, and it relies on many anachronistic examples to illustrate the case. Therefore, the book is inaccessible to all but the most dedicated students of type theory.

Enter Isabel Myers and mother, Katharine Briggs. Without their work, most people would know nothing of Jung's theory. Myers and Briggs made Jung's theory accessible to the masses by providing the four-letter codes, like ESTJ or INFP, that are now familiar to people all over the world. Though the pair did an excellent job simplifying the theory, their effort had the effect of taking Jung's type theory out of the broader context of his work. As a result, Myers and Briggs's efforts have weathered some harsh attacks that Jung's wider theory has not.

There are many reasons for this discrepancy, but chief among them is how common it is for people to disagree with descriptions of their type. That is hardly surprising because the descriptions are often caricatures based on the average appearance of the type, but appearances can be deceiving.

Some of those problems are unavoidable since it is impossible to boil an individual down to an average—quite the reverse because an average is based on a collection of individuals. While many do an adequate job of describing the average conscious behavior of each type, most descriptions neglect to account for the unconscious point of view, which to Jung, would be inexcusable because it is equivalent to describing half the person.

Jung seemed to believe the aspects of psychological typing in need of the most clarification were introversion and extraversion, even pointing out that while Freud's theories sufficiently accounted for the extraverted attitude and Adler's for the introverted, neither's theories could account for the totality of people's psychological experience. *Psychological Types*, therefore, devotes a great deal of energy to outlining the differences between introversion and extraversion, stating "the introverted standpoint is one which sets the ego and the subjective psychological process above the object and objective process," while "the extraverted standpoint, on the contrary, subordinates the subject to the object, so that the object has the higher value."[2] In comparison to introversion and extraversion, *Psychological Types* dedicates little time to the distinctions between sensation and intuition, or thinking and feeling.

Timely Types is the first in a series that tackles the nature of this "nothing" about which Socrates spoke—a series that explores this subject from both psychological and philosophical perspectives. The series will look back to what great minds have said on the subject and consider future implications because psychology and philosophy apply not only to the present time, but also the past and future.

The following chapters are a decidedly psychological look at Socrates's "nothing" and lay the groundwork for further investigation. Because *Timely Types* places oppositions at the center of its examination, it should be easy to grasp the foundations of type theory, which will be discussed comprehensively. Every cognitive function is treated in-depth as are introversion and extraversion. Unique about the type descriptions offered here is the way in which they are broken down. The introverted and extraverted psychologies are explored independently and only then united for complete descriptions—descriptions that account for every cognitive function's operation. In this way, Myers and Briggs's familiar terminology is kept intact, while allowing the descriptions to incorporate larger swaths of Jung's theory.

Following this thorough investigation, one will not only arrive at a complete understanding of type theory, but also will better know oneself and the world.

Theory of Psychological Types

"Who are you?" Despite all the niceties, this is the real question whenever meeting someone new; and because most people have never bothered asking themselves the question, it is easy to imagine a response like, "I'm Mike."

Some would take a more nuanced approach, identifying with their labels as lawyers, scientists, guidance counselors or even proud parents. Upon closer analysis, it is hard to deny that working a job or raising a child is anything more than a role that someone has; therefore, the question remains.

Some might say they are smart, or handsome, or passionate, maybe even cheerful. However, these are merely qualities people have; nothing more than ideas, really.

How can one resolve this dilemma? If a person is not what he does, nor his ideas about himself, what else is left? What about experience? Surely, everything a person is comes as the result of experience.

Getting warmer because experience plays an enormous role in shaping the way everyone sees the world. However, that answer seems to miss the mark because an experience is merely something one has encountered or lived through. If this is the answer to the question, however, who was it doing the "encountering" or "living through"? Certainly not one's experience.

Hence, an individual is not his experiences, not the roles he plays, not the wonderful qualities he might exhibit.

Every idea examined so far has at least one thing in common: each describes activities or ideas of the psyche. The psyche is not only the driving force behind every experience an individual has, it also permanently records each event. One's profession, no matter how labor intensive, is carried out by one's psyche.

Another word for the psyche is consciousness. If a person is consciousness at his core, perhaps all he must do is define consciousness to find the answer to who he is. Then again, it is the same difficulty encountered before because defining consciousness is like attempting to define who a person is. Alan Watts said, "Trying to define yourself is like trying to bite your own teeth."

The truth is, consciousness is a topic that defies even the most careful logical formulations because opposition is the apparent nature of consciousness.

According to the rules of logic, opposites cannot be reconciled; a statement cannot be both true and false, to give an example. That means any attempt to unite opposites cannot be done by thought, feeling or sensation; only intuition is capable of uniting opposites.

One example of the complexity surrounding this issue of the psyche's nature would be the age-old debate about its source — an issue that science has been unable to resolve conclusively.

Though the scientific consensus is that consciousness must arise from the brain, the hard evidence merely shows that consciousness functions at a subpar level when significant portions of the brain are damaged. That a damaged brain results in a decrease, or total loss, of consciousness was never in dispute. However, that evidence does nothing to disprove the possibility that consciousness arises outside the brain, which might simply be tuning into the consciousness "station." While quantum physics raises some ugly questions for the consensus view, everyone should be open to the truth, whatever it might be.

Though the psyche's complexity is well established, there is still good reason to believe a person is consciousness, while understanding that consciousness is impossible to define logically. A map is not the territory, a chair is simply a noun, not something people sit on; and those who attempt to define themselves are doing nothing less than forcing themselves into a psychological straightjacket. "It is astounding that man, the instigator, inventor, and vehicle of all these developments, the originator of all judgements and decisions and the planner of the future, must make himself such a *quantité negligeable*," said Jung.[3]

It might be wise, then, to discuss what is known of the psyche. It appears that everything that happens in consciousness is the result of four activities.

Everyone perceives the world either by means of his five senses or by intuiting the incorporeal aspects of reality; and each person judges either based on what he thinks or feels about an issue.

Jung called thought and feeling rational functions because they are used to form judgments. He referred to intuition and sensation as irrational functions since those functions do not judge, but only provide the content from which judgments are made. Rational and irrational do not mean what they often do in everyday speech, where rational decisions are ones devoid of feeling and irrational decisions fail to rely on proper logical reasoning.

Sensation, intuition, feeling and thinking are how people experience the world and themselves, as Jung laid out in his book, *Psychological Types*. The psyche expresses itself wholly in terms of those four aspects, meaning any competent psychological theory could be translated into Jung's theory of types.

Roughly speaking, sensation is the use of the five senses to gather information about the world and feeling is the value a person attaches to something; is it right or wrong, good or bad, pleasant or unpleasant? Thinking defines things by forming distinctions between true and false, and intuition is the ability to perceive the essence of things.

Sensation is the base factor of consciousness, wholly dependent on the other three factors of consciousness to be of any use in the human psyche. This should be obvious because a world in which there is no feeling, thought, or intuition would be unassimilable to the human mind. For one's sensations to have any consciousness, one needs to have some idea of what is being sensed, meaning the thinking function is essential to sensation's work. Similarly, people choose how to interact with the physical world largely based on feelings since the world would be an awfully boring place if everything had an equal value. One might be tempted to say that thought would be enough to navigate the physical world, but simple use of the thinking function would still leave each unit of physical reality with an equal valuation, thus meaning that there is no way to work out which physical stimulus is most worth pursuit. It would then be difficult to decide whether watching the beautiful sunset or securing food is most important, for example.

In the same way, feelings are dependent upon thought, for one cannot have a feeling about something without having some sense, however vague, of what that something is. The way one feels about a matter, how highly one rates a situation, these are completely dependent on the thoughts previously formed.

Lastly, thought can function based on the information that comes from sensations and feelings. But, no *original* thoughts can come from such data because thought imbues one's feelings and sensations with data in the first place. Therefore, from sensations and feelings, only thoughts that have already been thought, even unconsciously, may come. All original thoughts must come from intuition because thought, feeling and sensation are not able to perceive possibilities, which alone can be the source of that which has not yet been thought, felt or sensed. The fact that intuitives are quite fairly recognized for their ability to forecast trend lines and predict the future seems to confirm this idea.

Since intuition deals with possibilities, it must also deal with impossibilities, for something cannot be impossible if its impossibility is not possible, meaning that possibilities and impossibilities are one. Such convoluted language, though strange, should go a long way to explaining why intuition, alone, is able to reconcile oppositions. Language, as the primary instrument of thought, can only explain intuitive truths in roundabout ways. Since intuitive truths often deal with united opposites, any language used to describe a pair of opposites is habitually self-contradictory, almost no matter how carefully formed the language might be.

Thought determines *what is*, which thought can only do in contrast to *what is not*. If something were both so and not so, thought would be powerless to make any movement towards a conclusion. Similarly, since one cannot have feelings about something without cleaving that something from the things it is not, feelings also work in the world of oppositions. Finally, the oppositions in sensations have moved so far apart, that one is not able to recognize the oppositions' unity at all. One never sees light and dark together, or feels hot and cold at once, these opposites' unity can only be perceived intellectually, though once the intellectual weight of such a conclusion is worked fully into consciousness, it can certainly become part of the other processes.

Because dominant intuitives are, therefore, conscious of the widest field of data, it might be tempting to believe that they are more conscious or aware than other types. That, however, ignores the fact that intuitives must let many details slide between the cracks just because intuitives maintain such a focus on the big picture. If life were a mosaic, dominant intuitives would be attuned to the overall message of the mosaic but could very well fail to recognize the multitude of tiles making up the image. Dominant sensors, on the contrary, are intensely aware of the tiny details of life, yet struggle to maintain a view of the bigger picture just because of their mastery of the details. Therefore, dominant sensors would have no trouble seeing every detail in all the mosaic's tiles but might not notice that all those disparate tiles make up a larger whole with a cohesive meaning. Dominant thinkers and feelers would fall somewhere along the middle of those two extremes—where they fall depending on whether the dominant function is paired with auxiliary sensation or intuition.

Jung's recognition of these four fundamental parts of the psyche was nothing new, though he was the first to do it with such clarity. He was the only of psychology's big three—which also includes Freud and Adler—to handle this material in any depth.

His true innovation, however, was the addition of extraversion and introversion, which he called attitudes. Jung would argue that he did not discover the attitudes, merely elucidated them. While this is true, there is no question that he was the first to make the distinction intelligible to the masses.

Extraversion deals with the world objectively *because* it deals with objects in the outer world, and introversion is subjective because it is oriented to the subject, or inner world. Again, Jung did not equate objective with a logical thought process or subjective with an over attachment to feelings.

The combination of the attitudes with thinking, feeling, intuition and sensation forms the basis for his theory of types, and results in the realization of the cognitive functions; namely, extraverted and introverted sensation, extraverted and introverted feeling, extraverted and introverted thinking, and extraverted and introverted intuition. From these cognitive functions are derived eight *primary* types, one example being the introverted feeling type.

Because consciousness is composed of oppositions, it must follow that several dichotomies form the basis of the theory. The introverted attitude is opposed to the extraverted, as are thinking to feeling and intuition to sensation. The following chart will help one remember these dichotomies:

EXTRAVERSION	INTROVERSION
SENSATION	INTUITION
FEELING	THINKING

These dichotomies, found by reading horizontally across the table, form the basis of the theory.

Those who already have experience with psychological types have noticed that the judging/perceiving axis has not been mentioned. The reason is, judgment and perception, as a separate and distinct axis, are not original parts of Jung's work. It is not that the human psyche lacks judgment and perception; rather, it was previously noted that feeling and thought are judgment processes, while sensation and intuition relate to perception. Thus, the addition of a separate judgment/perception dichotomy might be useful in the context of popular psychology, but its inclusion is completely redundant. This additional judgment and perception opposition simply tells a person what side each type shows the world, but what one sees is not always what one gets.

As for the cognitive functions, all people use each to varying degrees, though only four cognitive functions are conscious to any degree.

One's preferences for some cognitive functions over others is not subject to change; those preferences are merely expressed differently based on one's environment and circumstances. This is a necessity of the theory because any attempt to change preferences would result in a complete and total upheaval of the psyche, the kind that would most likely result in time spent in a psychiatric ward. The best a person can do is bring greater balance to these dichotomies.

Why? It goes back to the split between the conscious and unconscious parts of the psyche.

One of the cognitive functions, generally known as the dominant function, takes on the role of ego, the ego being the center of the conscious mind.[4] The dominant function always stands opposed to a largely undifferentiated and somewhat unconscious inferior function; the inferior function being the weakest function and the one in which the outlines of a person's shadow first start to come into relief; shadow[5] because it consists of material that is largely anathema to the conscious point of view–though the importance of the material in the unconscious cannot be overstated.

DOMINANT FUNCTION
INFERIOR FUNCTION

If the dominant function is perception, so is the inferior. If the dominant function is a judging function, so is the inferior.

Despite its repression, the viewpoint of the inferior function is the fuel that allows the dominant function to do its work. As a result, if the dominant function is an extraverted judging function, it is necessary that the opposing introverted judging function be the inferior function (e.g., dominant extraverted feeling opposed to inferior introverted thinking).

Further, the dominant function always has an auxiliary cognitive function that compensates for the dominant's inherent one-sidedness. The auxiliary relieves some of the pressure built up by the inferior function because the auxiliary and inferior functions always share the same attitude, i.e., introversion and extraversion. The dominant function always differs from the auxiliary in every regard. Therefore, dominant introverted sensing would pair with either extraverted feeling or extraverted thinking as its auxiliary.

| DOMINANT FUNCTION | AUXILIARY FUNCTION |

The dominant and auxiliary differ in every respect. If the dominant function is introverted perception, the auxiliary must be extraverted judgment, for example.

Like the dominant function, the inferior function also has an auxiliary function through which the inferior attempts to voice its views to the conscious mind. The inferior function's auxiliary process is called the tertiary function. The tertiary function always opposes the inferior in every respect, just as the dominant does the auxiliary. Therefore, if the inferior function were extraverted feeling, the tertiary process would either be introverted sensation or introverted intuition.

| TERTIARY FUNCTION | INFERIOR FUNCTION |

The tertiary and inferior functions also differ in every respect.

Because the attitude of the dominant and tertiary functions is the same, the tertiary function is more conscious for its user than the inferior function. Moreover, the tertiary and auxiliary functions share the same relationship to each other that the dominant function shares with the inferior, except the auxiliary does not dominate the tertiary function to the same extent.

| AUXILIARY FUNCTION |
| TERTIARY FUNCTION |

If the auxiliary function is perception, so is the tertiary. If the auxiliary function is a judging function, so is the tertiary.

The following chart, representative of ISFP, is an example of how all these pieces interact. In this case, the two lighter boxes stand for introversion, while the darker boxes indicate extraversion (the reverse would be true of an extravert); the solid shading of the dominant and inferior functions represents their polar relationship, while the patterned shading of the auxiliary and tertiary represents their polarity.

DOMINANT INTROVERTED FEELING	AUXILIARY EXTRAVERTED SENSATION
TERTIARY INTROVERTED INTUITION	INFERIOR EXTRAVETED THINKING

When one considers the complexity involved, a true change of psychological type seems most implausible; conscious and unconscious minds would be thrown into a state of chaos. Even a semi-permanent switch from the dominant to the auxiliary function would be dubious because it also would mean swapping the position of the unconscious; and how does one swap the position of the unconscious when it is something that, by its very nature, most people can barely see or acknowledge, much less understand?

Jung thought a change of types would be implausible for somewhat varied reasons. In *Psychological Types* he wrote, "I do not think it improbable, in view of one's experience that a reversal of type often proves exceedingly harmful to the physiological well-being of the organism, usually causing acute exhaustion."[6]

Development of the conscious mind is a gradual process. Roughly the first 15 years of life are spent developing the dominant function, and the next 15 mastering the auxiliary, which when combined, constitute a person's ego block. Should the ego fail to strengthen itself to a sufficient degree, one would encounter a person who is ill equipped to overcome many of life's basic struggles. It is not until the age of 30 that most people even begin to gain any consciousness of their tertiary function, and during the next 10 years or more, most are struggling to gain some degree of integration between the auxiliary and tertiary functions. There are exceptions, of course, and if a person is taking time to read a book about psychological types, that person is probably one of those exceptions.

Unfortunately, most never gain any level of conscious mastery over their inferior function because it requires intense introspection and no small portion of self-honesty; instead, most are subjected to the inferior's apparent whims as it struggles to achieve sufficient integration into the conscious psyche.

The less conscious one is of a cognitive function's operations, the more the function operates according to the rules of collective consciousness. To illustrate, the typical person using inferior extraverted thinking would depend on authoritative sources and scientific consensus for factual evidence. Someone with dominant extraverted thinking would not only better discriminate whether authoritative sources are helpful or not, but also have a greater ability to assess the validity of the information from a factual standpoint.

The basic framework of Jung's type theory has now been outlined, but to master the theory, it is necessary to dive deeper into introversion and extraversion. Just remember the following:

- The psyche uses four processes to operate in the world: sensation, feeling, thinking and intuition

- Sensation and intuition are opposing perceptive processes, while feeling and thinking are opposing judging processes
- All mentally healthy people have some degree of conscious access to each of those four processes
- Because of the oppositional nature of the psyche, skill at one process means deficiency at another
- Two of those four processes are always extraverted, while two are always introverted
- Most people will be good at one introverted process and one extraverted process, while displaying weakness with the opposing processes. That means that there are two strong processes and two weak ones
  - Both the dominant and auxiliary functions are strong
  - Both the inferior and tertiary functions are weak
- The dominant function always opposes the inferior, while the auxiliary always opposes the tertiary
- Hence, use of one function necessitates the use of its opposite
  - Introverted thought always opposes extraverted feeling, for example
- One cannot function in the world without both perception and judgment, as well as introversion and extraversion
- Therefore, the dominant and auxiliary functions always differ in every regard
  - Introverted dominant functions demand an extraverted auxiliary, and vice versa

- Judging dominant functions demand a perceiving auxiliary, and vice versa
- The same principle is true of the inferior and tertiary functions
- In addition to their four preferred functions, all types unconsciously use the other four. Because their use is unconscious, these functions are often called shadow functions
- From the combination of the above, the now-famous four-letter codes are derived
  - "E" stands for extraversion, while "I" stands for introversion
  - "N" stands for iNtuition, while "S" stands for sensing
  - "F" stands for feeling and "T" stands for thinking
  - "J" for judging and "P" for perceiving
- There are 16 types, two for each dominant cognitive function

Extraversion, Introversion and Libido

Even though it took Jung more than 300 pages to elucidate what he meant by their use, the words introversion and extraversion have become so common that most people have at least some idea what the two terms mean, even without the framework laid out in *Psychological Types*.

In the everyday world, one can find many different attitudes to life. Despite a multitude of viewpoints, there are differences that are typical.

Some people are happiest interacting with a small circle of close friends or family, if anyone at all; others love the thrill and excitement of meeting and interacting with new people. Some like to unwind by going out for a night on the town, enjoying the loud music almost as much as the dancing; others might prefer the quiet of their home, a glass of wine and a nice book.

There are those who constantly consider what others think of their career, the way they dress or the family car, constantly adjusting their behavior to the world's standards. There are others who could care less about the world's standards and who would sooner demand that the entire world change than make the adjustments needed to fit in better as an individual. Some do their best thinking by taking some time to introspect and others do their best thinking by talking things through with others and refining their ideas based on feedback.

All people are both introverted and extraverted. Lacking any extraversion, the introvert would literally be mute and fail to register any details of the outside world. The extravert, on the other hand, would be worse off than a robot if he lacked introversion because there would be nobody home to assimilate his rich experience of the world; at least many robots can record their experiences.

Myers gave the clearest explanation:

> A good way to visualize the difference is to think of the dominant process as the General and the auxiliary process as his Aide. In the case of the extravert, the General is always out in the open. Other people meet him immediately and do their business directly with him. They can get the official viewpoint on anything at any time. The Aide stands respectfully in the background or disappears inside the tent. The introvert's General is inside the tent, working on matters of top priority. The Aide is outside fending off interruptions, or, if he is inside helping the General, he comes out to see what is wanted. It is the Aide whom others meet and with whom they do their business. Only when the business is very important (or the friendship is very close) do others get in to see the General himself.[7]

It is not quite accurate that the introvert's General comes out for important business or even for close friendships, so it is important to exercise a bit of caution.

Because introverted functions are directed purely towards the inner world, only the person using them is privy to the functions' inner essence; from a purely logical standpoint, it is possible to gauge another person's inner reality only by implication, not by direct experience. Moreover, introversion and extraversion do not form an independent axis in type theory, despite how things might seem in Myers and Briggs's system.

When a person observes the world, for example, he never finds extraversion or introversion apart from the four activities of consciousness, which are intuition, thought, feeling and sensing. Neither would he find the four activities apart from the attitudes of introversion and extraversion. Someone whose dominant function is introverted sensing is an introvert only because her dominant function is introverted. A person who utilizes dominant extraverted feeling is an extravert owing to his chief cognitive function being extraverted.

It is nonetheless necessary to discuss introversion and extraversion as distinct from the cognitive functions to shed light upon the pair's role in the human psyche.

When one digs deeply enough into each of the cognitive functions, it becomes clear that there is no real difference between the introverted and extraverted processes. That is, thinking aims to determine what is true or false regardless of the attitude in which it is used, and the same is true for the other three factors of consciousness.

The difference between a function in its extraverted or introverted attitude ultimately comes down to libido and the direction in which it flows.

No, not the libido people hear about on television commercials that advertise blue pills, neither is it Sigmund Freud's concept of libido, which centered on an internal, instinctual force that is often repressed, unconscious and related to sexuality.

To Jung, libido was the psyche's energy saying, "There is no energy unless there is a tension of opposites; hence it is necessary to discover the opposite to the attitude of the conscious mind."[8] The extravert is always pouring out libido from himself to the object, whereas the introvert is always withdrawing energy from the object to himself. Looked at another way, introverts focus on their inner worlds, which Jung called the subjective factor because it refers to the subject of one's experience: oneself. On the other hand, extraverts focus on the objective factor, or the outer world.

Though Jung, Myers and Briggs did not lay it out in their own outlines of type theory, the introvert's inpouring and the extravert's outpouring of libido could also be understood in terms of the ancient, unresolved argument about universals and particulars.

When a person sees a green truck, he is seeing a particular truck that happens to be green. It is particular since it is a single truck that he registers with his senses, i.e., the truck has a reality that is undeniably physical. Thus, particulars can only occupy one portion of space-time at any given moment, and are therefore, non-repeatable.

However, all particulars contain certain qualities that, on some level, seem to exist independent of the particular because those qualities can exist in many places at one time, and these are universals. For example, the truck's greenness is not only a property of that particular truck; it also describes other green trucks, trees, grass and any other number of things that are green. How is it, then, that green, which is the color of this particular truck, can exist non-locally, i.e., in many distinct places at once? While one can observe universal qualities within a particular, universals' non-locality indicates that their reality is not physical, but psychic.

The goal here is not to resolve this never-ending dilemma; rather, the point is to use basic knowledge of universals and particulars to better understand the natures of introversion and extraversion.

The introverted tendency is to operate from universals; the extraverted way is to operate based on particulars.

If introversion focuses on universals, why does each introvert seem to be unique? Well, one never finds introversion without extraversion, i.e., introversion and extraversion are two sides of the same coin. Thus, extraversion's link to particulars, conditions the introvert's universal view, resulting in a unique personality. Just as introversion prevents the extravert from adjusting to the point of total identity with an object such as a rock, extraversion keeps the introvert from over adjusting to psychic ideals.

Someone who uses introverted thinking is not aiming to determine what is true or false about a particular circumstance, but to extract from that circumstance laws that all similar circumstances must obey. The introverted thinker would argue that one is better able to deal with all particular cases if one understands the universal rules. The extraverted thinker, on the other hand, has little interest in defining universal laws regarding a particular circumstance, but instead concerns himself with how to manipulate a particular situation to his end; the extraverted thinker would argue that every particular circumstance is unique, so attempting to abstract universal law from each event is not only preposterous, but slows down the action.

Where the introverted feeler is concerned with the universal meaning of good and bad, the extraverted feeler is concerned purely with what is good or bad in a particular case. As a result, the extraverted feeler would find that what is good or bad changes from situation to situation, whereas the introverted feeler would arrive at a more complete, but also more static view.

This is a necessary result because the extraverted viewpoint deals always with the outer world; and because one can never be in all places at all times, one invariably encounters only particulars when looking outside of oneself.

The introvert, however, looks inwardly to the psyche, and because the psyche, at its greatest depths, is the balancer of all opposites, the resulting viewpoint must relate to universals. Nothing is more unlike light than darkness, for at light's presence darkness flees. Therefore, anything else a person could compare to light must bear more resemblance to light than does darkness. It would not be unreasonable to conclude, then, that the psyche must be universal in its scope since an infinitely divisible spectrum exists in between any two opposing points. Indeed, the psyche could be likened to a hard drive, and despite thousands of years of files being written to it, the hard drive's capacity does not appear to be diminished in the least.

There is a long history of likening consciousness to a circle or sphere. Even Jung wrote voluminously about mandalas, which are representations of the Self,[9] generally as a squared circle.[10] In the context of type theory, the importance of mandalas can hardly be overstated. The circle represents totality, whereas the square has four points that make up two oppositions. The circle would represent Self, and the two oppositions would represent thinking opposed to feeling, and sensation as opposed to intuition.

In the previous example, if light is one point on the circle's circumference, darkness would occupy the farthest possible point away from light.

Just as all people are both introverts and extraverts, everyone relies on universals and particulars in understanding and interacting with the world. Accordingly, introverted and extraverted types only emerge owing to habitual preference for one attitude over the other.

Because of the opposing focus on universals or particulars, there are some common frustrations between introverts and extraverts.

The extravert finds that the introvert often ignores the reality of the objective situation. The introvert complains about her job prospects, but the extravert rolls his eyes because the introvert refuses to engage in social networking or consider going back to school; the introvert is upset because she does not have good relationships, but the extravert finds it confounding because the introvert never tries to open to her colleagues.

On the other hand, the introvert sometimes concludes that the extraverted style is shallow. The extravert is shocked that his plan did not turn out as expected, but the introvert sees that the disaster would have been easy to spot if there had been more introspection. The extravert does not understand why his classmates will not trust him, but the introvert sees that the extravert being too willing to say what everyone wants to hear makes his classmates question his integrity.

Since it is only by means of the interaction between introversion and extraversion that one can arrive at any estimation of who one is as an individual, it is necessary to discuss not only the extravert's and introvert's outer appearances, but also their inner natures. It is also important to discuss the nature of both attitudes from the perspective of both the conscious and unconscious minds.

Extraversion

Extraversion is the outpouring of libido upon particular objects or experiences. As a result, extraverts tend to feel energized by interacting with the world in concrete ways. The extra libido flowing to the extravert's conscious viewpoint results in less libido flowing to the unconscious, subjective psyche, which compensates for the conscious extraverted attitude.

People sense, understand and manipulate the outer world through extraversion. There can be no self-aware subject without objects, for it is only in relation to the objects of one's experience that one can distinguish oneself; and because the conscious and unconscious minds stand in an opposing yet compensatory relationship, one cannot refine one's inner wisdom without the crucible of objective existence. For example, it is impossible to formulate theories or have any sense of history without facts and data.

It is through extraversion alone, that humanity can come to any sort of consensus about the nature of reality. Unlike the inner world, which is directly accessible only to its owner, all readily experience the outer world and generally arrive at far-reaching agreement about their observations; and obviously, any effort to engineer changes within society must work through extraverted processes.

Since the outer world is made up of particular objects, and because each object is unique and non-repeatable, extraversion demands greater adaptability to the outer world. Extraverts like to act then think. Because the extravert naturally attunes to the objective situation, his decisions and actions always bear a clear relation to the objective reality, even if it results in a degree of self-alienation. Inner truths influence the extravert less than the objective situation because he never expects to find truth within, only without. The reality of the outer world directs and conditions the extravert's views.

"His life makes it perfectly clear that it is the object and not this subjective view that plays the determining role in his consciousness. Naturally he has subjective views too, but their determining value is less than that of the objective conditions," said Jung of the extravert.[11]

Extraverts believe that by taking on many subjects, relationships and experiences, they can come to understand any subject, relationship or experience; and it is this outwardly derived understanding that governs the extravert's inner life.

One word that characterizes the extraverted attitude, therefore, is breadth. Compared to his introverted counterpart, the extravert will typically have a wider circle of friends, interests and hobbies because particular experiences are what excite the extravert most. Where the introvert is happy to dig deeply into a small number of topics and relationships, the extravert is liable to feel as if he is locked in a cage.

If the conscious, extraverted attitude stays within a normal range, the extravert is unlikely to experience an internal disturbance that results from too little libido flowing to the unconscious mind. However, when the extravert fails to allow room for the introversion that naturally bubbles up from his unconscious, the unconscious begins lashing out by any means necessary to restore a sense of balance to the whole psyche.

Extraversion taken too far, often means that the extravert repeats mistakes because there is insufficient reflection to allow him to consciously correct issues. One then finds a situation in which the subject feels powerless to resist the influence of the object. That is, the extravert's adaptability, which had before been a strength, becomes an unbearable weakness. The extravert then lacks any inner compass for deciding between right and wrong, or true and false, instead relying exclusively on outside authority to make those determinations.

The extravert loses out because his dependence on particulars can lead him to miss the universal insights that would allow him to better gauge the underlying patterns of phenomenal existence.

The more the extravert dams libido off from his unconscious mind, the more often he will lose himself in objective experience and the more gullible he will become. Others will find that the extravert has taken on characteristics that could best be described as youthfully haughty and prejudiced. Hysteria will set in if the extravert does not allow the unconscious to re-establish the psyche's balance.

> A purely objective orientation does violence to a multitude of subjective impulses, intentions, needs, and desires and deprives them of the libido that is their natural right. Man is not a machine than can be remodeled for quite other purposes as occasion demands, in the hope that it will go on functioning as regularly as before but in a quite different way. He carries his whole history with him; in his very structure is written the history of mankind. This historical element in man represents a vital need to which a wise psychic economy must respond.[12]

The extravert's greatest risk regarding his natural introversion is never that he gives too much ground to the introverted viewpoint, but that he is too willing to forsake himself and his needs for the sake of the object. As a result, the extravert's unconscious mind is egotistical.

It is no wonder, then, that the extravert, who genuinely believes that he is giving himself up for the sake of the object, is sometimes viewed with a degree of mistrust regarding the sincerity and durability of his words. Imagine the extraverted boss who tells his employees that the whole team will be going to a company-sponsored conference next month, so the employees should put in extra hours to put on a great show. His employees recognize that their good work is, by definition, their boss's good work. Thus, while the extraverted boss could honestly be seeking to help his employees' careers, he might not realize how self-serving his behavior really is.

Extraverts can avoid the results of an imbalance between introversion and extraversion by affirming the importance and value of their inner experience and wisdom and utilizing that insight in their interactions with the world.

Introversion

Introversion is the inpouring of libido upon universal and timeless parts of the psyche, namely the world of archetypes. As a result, introverts gain energy by refining their inner worlds. The extra libido flowing to the introvert's conscious mind comes at the expense of less libido flowing to her extraverted, unconscious mind, which stands in compensatory relation to the conscious viewpoint.

Of the world of archetypes, Jung gave this explanation:

There are as many archetypes as there are typical situations in life. Endless repetition has engraved these experiences into our psychic constitution, not in the form of images filled with content, but at first only as *forms without content*, representing merely the possibility of a certain type of perception and action. When a situation occurs which corresponds to a given archetype, that archetype becomes activated.[13]

Introversion allows one to see, experience and understand oneself. There are no objects to experience without a subject because all experiences require a subject to experience them; since the introverted and extraverted attitudes compensate one another, personal insight and inner guidance can help people better execute in the outer world. A person cannot systematize processes or improve her friendships without the input that comes from the introverted functions; neither can someone remain open to the outer world and its possibilities without the subject concluding that remaining open-minded has served her well.

"Although the introverted consciousness is naturally aware of external conditions, it selects the subjective determinants as the decisive ones," said Jung.[14]

Unlike the outer world, which is directly accessible to anyone, only the subject can see directly the psyche's direction, goals and desires. As a result, society is completely powerless to alter the individual's self-perception without the individual's agreement, whether agreement is given consciously or unconsciously.

Because people's sense of who they are comes from within, introverts tend to exhibit more self-awareness and awareness of the motivations behind their actions than extraverts do. Introverts like to think then act. When addressing problems, introverts are much more likely to take time to reflect and, only then, proceed based on that reflection. Since the introvert is clearly oriented toward her subjective experience, her decisions and actions always bear a clear relation to her inner desires and universal understandings, even if the response seems to ignore the outer reality of the situation. Objective situations influence the introvert less than what the objective situation brings forth within her psyche since, for her, the individual purpose is most important.

The introvert often believes that by introspecting about a few subjects, relationships or experiences, a person ends up understanding the framework of all subjects, relationships and experiences. It is by these inwardly derived frameworks that most introverts interact with the outer world.

A good word to describe the introverted attitude is depth. In comparison to the extravert, the introvert has little interest in friendships or hobbies that she is not able to absorb thoroughly because the introvert is most stimulated by arriving at universally applicable understandings. Where the extravert is thrilled to hop from experience to experience, the introvert is likely to feel as if there is too much jam and not enough toast.

If the introverted point of view stays within a healthy range, the introvert is unlikely to suffer from decreased libido flowing to the unconscious. When the introvert fails to allow room to express the extraversion rising from her unconscious mind, however, the unconscious begins acting out in any way necessary to restore balance between the introverted and extraverted attitudes.

When taken to the extreme, the introvert's reliance on reflection leads to her missing opportunities and experiences that would enrich her point of view. One then finds a situation in which the object is powerless to force needed change in the introvert. That is, the introvert's strong sense of self, which had before been a strength, becomes a near-fatal weakness. The introvert will then make poorly tuned decisions for the objective situation because of an over-reliance on her inner compass for direction.

The introvert sometimes drops the ball since her faith in universals leads to her forgetting that each particular is unique and demands a distinctive response.

The more the introvert walls off her unconscious mind from the libido to which it is entitled, the more she will find that she has lost touch with reality and the more she will find herself utilizing a dogged egoism to fend off the objective situation. Objective experience will become more and more unbearable until a change in the subjective influence allows libido to flow to the unconscious mind. If the unconscious mind is unable to nudge the introvert towards a healthier balance, it is likely that neurosis will set in.

Because unconscious cognitive functions tend to be unpolished, the introvert has a brand of extraversion that is far rawer than encountered in the extravert. Jung says the following:

> The predominance of the subjective factor in consciousness naturally involves a devaluation of the object. The object is not given the importance that belongs to it by right. Just as it plays too great a role in the extraverted attitude, it has too little meaning for the introvert.[15]

Jung believed that the introvert's greatest danger regarding extraversion was not due to her introversion, but due to the natural tendency to make the ego the center of her experience, a tendency that is unconscious in extraverts. The ego,[16] which is merely the center of the *conscious* mind, is too fragile to form a balanced opposition to the outer world. However, Jung viewed the Self, which is the center of *both the conscious and unconscious psyche*, as commensurable with the totality of objective existence.[17] It is the Self — the balancer of the most significant opposition in the human mind, consciousness and unconsciousness — that is universal in scope.

Should egoism reign in the introverted psyche, the ego will become enslaved to objective data. Change and transformation become terrifying, objects take on larger-than-life characteristics and the introvert loses all ability to relate to her environment in healthy ways.

The introvert can maintain a harmonious balance between her introversion and extraversion by remaining flexible in her objective considerations and reminding herself that it is acceptable to remain in the here and now.

While it is true that all people can be divided into two types, introverted and extraverted, it is also true that within those groups, there is extensive psychological diversity. It is necessary, therefore, to delve into the nature of each cognitive function.

The Cognitive Functions
In-Depth

Though the bulk of type theory has been outlined, a complete investigation of psychological typing demands a thorough exploration of all eight cognitive functions. The cognitive functions form the backbone of Jung's theory, so grasping the cognitive functions not only improves self-awareness, but also provides the tools needed to discern others' views of the world.

Just as the introversion-extraversion axis discussed as a stand-alone entity makes for nothing more than theoretical discussion, so too does the investigation of any of the cognitive functions in isolation; for owing to the nature of the psyche, which consists of both conscious and unconscious aspects, one can never posit a thing without positing its opposite, at least implicitly. Thus, while it is necessary to learn about each cognitive function separately to understand its unique function in the psyche, in reality, there is nothing more than a judgment dichotomy and a perception dichotomy; it is only from the distribution of introversion and extraversion within those two dichotomies that the cognitive functions emerge for theoretical consideration.

Simply stated, thinking and feeling are two poles of a single process called judgment; sensing and intuition are two poles of a single process called perception. One's perceptions will be lacking if the perceptions do not allow room for both sensing and intuition; similarly, one's judgment will prove ineffective if there is insufficient space for both thinking and feeling. Not only does each process depend on both factors of consciousness, each also requires particulars and universals, i.e., extraversion and introversion, to provide the toolbox needed for successful assimilation to the world.

It should not be surprising, therefore, that littered throughout Jung's writings is the word enantiodromia. Enantiodromia describes the tendency of things, both physical and psychic, to become their opposites, especially when the viewpoint is extreme or unreasonable. Though this tendency might sound magical and bizarre, it is nonetheless real, and a failure to balance both sides of each dichotomy leaves one open to experiencing enantiodromias of the most extreme kind.

At a concrete level, one can see this never-ending interplay of opposites in the way night tends to become day, dry tends to become moist, high tide tends to become low tide, and things that use to be symbols of innovation tend to become symbols of stagnation. Isaac Newton also saw enantiodromia at work when he said, "To every action there is always an equal and opposite reaction."

A few mild examples might clarify the concept of enantiodromia at the psychic level. In the summer of 2010, professional basketball player, LeBron James, decided to leave his team in Cleveland to join forces with his friends Chris Bosh and Dwyane Wade on the Miami Heat. Because of the overwhelming talent advantage such a roster had, sports media and many fans spent the next few years excoriating James for his move—using the up-and-coming Kevin Durant's humility and commitment to his team as foils to undermine James's character.

Then came the summer of 2016, in which Kevin Durant left his Oklahoma City team under similar circumstances seen when James left Cleveland, except the talent discrepancy between Durant's new team, the Golden State Warriors, and the rest of the league was even greater than what Miami had with Bosh, Wade and James. Throw in the fact that the roster Durant left behind was superior to the team James left behind, with Durant's team overwhelmingly favored to beat the Golden State Warriors after accumulating a 3-1 series advantage in the 2016 Western Conference Finals, and all the makings of a controversy were in place.

Many who supported James's move to Miami were outraged that Kevin Durant would join forces not only with the team he lost to after being favored to win, but also with a team that was one quarter away from winning a championship the previous season. Many who supported Durant's move as being the best for his career were among James's critics when he switched teams for the same reason. Herein lies an enantiodromia, which has a strange way of balancing out the one-sidedness of opposites.

Another example is the United States' 2016 presidential election. When Barack Obama first came to office, most Americans were fans of his deliberative approach to running government and his appeals to hope. After eight years of such a style, many Americans hungered for a president, like Donald Trump, who embraced spontaneity in his decision-making process and was willing to appeal to Americans' legitimate fears. Obama spoke of taking the country in a new direction. Trump's campaign was based on the idea that America's greatest days are behind her. Just as Obama and the Democrats' effort to pass healthcare reform was met with angry protests in town halls across America, Trump and the Republican's plan to repeal the Affordable Care Act was met with equal dissent. If one style is good, the other must be bad, yet Americans felt that both approaches could make for a successful presidency. Again, this is an example of an enantiodromia restoring balance to the conscious viewpoint but, in these cases, the enantiodromias applied to a whole nation instead of a single person.

As previously indicated, every person consciously uses four cognitive functions. In general, one of the functions is very well developed, acting as a person's default approach to life. That function is called the dominant function. People feel quite comfortable using their dominant function, utilizing it to solve many of life's problems, sometimes problems for which that particular function is not the best approach. The auxiliary function assists the dominant function by filling in for the dominant function's weaknesses. The dominant and auxiliary functions always differ in every regard. Thus, if the dominant process is perception, the auxiliary function is judgment, and vice versa. If the dominant process is extraverted, the auxiliary must be introverted.

The auxiliary function is typically well developed in most adults, with introverts more likely to gain some facility with the auxiliary process early in life because introverts need some way to interact with the outside world. Extraverts, while having greater ease in the outer world from the outset, do not typically begin developing their auxiliary function until they begin to feel the necessity of self-reflection.

Then there is the tertiary function, which balances out the auxiliary process. When the auxiliary process is judgment, the tertiary function is the opposing judging function; when the auxiliary process is a perception process, the tertiary function is always the opposing perceiving function.

If the dominant process is someone in the prime of her life, and the auxiliary is the student who is about to graduate from college, the tertiary function is an adolescent; and like adolescents, a handful of people have well-developed tertiary functions, but in general, the immaturity is palpable.

Last, is the inferior function. If the dominant function is a perceiving process, the inferior is always the opposing perceiving process, and the same principle would apply if judgment were the dominant function.

Most people ignore their inferior function because it is existentially opposed to their preferred way of operating, which is through the dominant function. Thus, the inferior function is the toddler of the bunch. Like toddlers, the inferior function has a rudimentary comprehension of the world, but still requires grownups — the more developed functions — to ensure its survival.

The inferior function, though largely unconscious, still provides information of the utmost importance to an individual's wellbeing. Someone with inferior sensing could not comprehend physical reality if the inferior function were completely unconscious, for example. The inferior function contributes content to the conscious viewpoint, but the inferior's scope, depth and breadth of insight are quite restricted and coarse when compared to its abilities when in the dominant or auxiliary positions.

There are two perception dichotomies, one using a combination of introverted intuition and extraverted sensation, and another using extraverted intuition and introverted sensation. Everyone consciously uses one perception dichotomy or the other.

Similarly, there are two judgment dichotomies. One relies on introverted feeling and extraverted thinking, and the other relies on extraverted feeling and introverted thinking.

Any combination of these dichotomies gives the potential to operate successfully in the world and forge consensus, but clear epistemological distinctions emerge. Someone who prefers sensing to intuition likely has a different view of the world than one who prefers intuition to sensing. Someone who uses introverted feeling and extraverted thinking will typically have a much different view of the world than someone who prefers extraverted feeling and introverted thinking, and this does not factor in the perceiving dichotomies, which would result in even more distinctions.

These distinctions, when well handled, enrich everyone's experience of life. On the other hand, these distinctions have often resulted in conflicts that have recurred since time immemorial.

It follows, then, that a clear understanding of not only each dichotomy, but also each cognitive function paves the way for happier living by allowing people to bring greater balance to their lives.

Though it is not necessary for the following analysis, some might like to know how to derive a type's cognitive functions from the familiar four-letter codes. From the following formula, one can understand how it is done:

- The middle two letters in any type's code describe the two best functions

- ENTJ's best functions are intuition and thinking, while ISFP's two best are sensing and feeling
- The last letter, P or J, describes which function is extraverted, the perceptive function or the judging function
  - Thus, ENTJ extravert their judging process: thinking. ISFP, on the contrary, extravert their perceptive process: sensation
- The two top functions can now be placed in the correct order by looking at the E-I dichotomy
  - Because ENTJ are extraverts, their extraverted process must be the dominant function, while their introverted function must be the auxiliary. Hence, ENTJ use extraverted thinking as their dominant function, and introverted intuition as their auxiliary process
  - Because ISFP are introverts, their introverted process must be the dominant function, while their extraverted process must be the auxiliary. Therefore, ISFP use introverted feeling as their dominant function and extraverted sensation as their auxiliary
- The law of psychological opposition can now be applied
  - Because ENTJ use dominant extraverted thinking, they must also use inferior introverted feeling; and since this type uses auxiliary introverted intuition, ENTJ must also use tertiary extraverted sensation

- Since ISFP's dominant function is introverted feeling, their inferior function must be extraverted thinking; and because ISFP use auxiliary extraverted sensation they must also use tertiary introverted intuition

Perception

Extraverted Sensation-Introverted Intuition Axis

Within the Se-Ni, or extraverted sensation-introverted intuition dichotomy, are those who prefer Se over Ni and others who prefer Ni over Se.

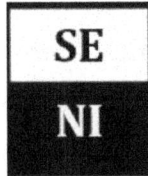

Extraverted sensation and introverted intuition are always opposed to each other, showing that each function is part of a larger process.

Se-Ni types perceive physical reality in a concrete, collective manner directly focused on particular objects in the outer world; their sensory experience lies outside of them. On the other hand, meaning is found within.

To Se-Ni types, meaning can be argued since everyone holds a unique point of view, but there can be no argument about physical experience and real-world events.

This is because Se assimilates to the object, thereby minimizing one's unique sensory experience in favor of maximizing the collective's. In those who prefer Se to Ni, this point of view is decisive, and it weds these people to a deeply concrete and literal experience of reality.

In those who prefer Ni to Se, one finds the opposite tendency because Ni relates objective experience to the subject in a cohesive way: through one's psyche. Thus, a strong introverted intuitive might identify the perfect time to act on a plan by receiving a vision of what the opportune moment will look like.

Ni could not map meaning onto the outer world without awareness of the world, so Se is fundamental to Ni.

Se would not truly be aware of the world if it had no idea what an experience or object means, so Ni is fundamental to Se. To give a rudimentary instance of this interaction between Se and Ni, a dog always recognizes its owner and has some sense of the owner's relationship to it, however vague that sense might be. No matter how many people the dog might encounter, the dog knows that its owner has a meaning that is unique to it. As is the case with any perception, one can interpret the dog's behavior through a Si-Ne perspective as well.

People who prefer this dichotomy are quite open to new and novel physical experience, especially if Se is preferred to Ni; but Se-Ni types tend to demonstrate greater caution than their Si-Ne counterparts in maintaining their psychic equilibrium, and they demonstrate that caution with their incredible preparedness for life's psychic experiences. This tendency is, of course, highlighted in those who prefer Ni to Se.

Se-Ni types outwardly appear to be more centered and focused than Si-Ne types because Se-Ni always has an eye toward the observable world. Inwardly, the situation is reversed because Se-Ni types' inner psychologies are oriented towards the universals of psychic experience, which tends to make the inner world subtle and a bit amorphous.

Compared to Si-Ne types, Se-Ni types show economy of communication, usually displaying less verbal ease (especially the introverts) but packing more meaning into each word than Si-Ne types because meaning runs so deep for Se-Ni types.

Extraverted Sensing

Dominant: ESFP, ESTP
Auxiliary: ISFP, ISTP
Tertiary: ENFJ, ENTJ
Inferior: INFJ, INTJ

Extraverted sensation, or Se, is one of the four extraverted functions and one of four perceiving functions all people use.

Like introverted sensation, Se allows one to utilize one's five senses to understand and interact with physical reality. Unlike introverted sensation, Se does not form an internal map of past sensory experience, comparing current experiences to those had in the past. Instead, Se is highly attuned to the external environment and it tends to focus on whatever it perceives to be the strongest stimulus. Se is less concerned about the effect the observable world has on individuals.

Where Se craves new and novel experiences, believing the here-and-now is all that matters, introverted sensation likes things to stay the way they have always been. This is because Se does a fantastic job tuning into the outer world, but fails to tune into its subjective sensory experience, which is introverted sensing's domain. As a result, introverted sensation prioritizes bodily comfort in a way that Se does not.

Since Se is oriented to the objective factor, it tends to take things at face value, while introverted sensors focus on what sense experience is like *to them*. Jung gave a great example to illustrate this difference.[18] Imagine a group of people at the Grand Canyon attempting to paint exactly what each sees. Once the would-be painters get past their technical abilities or limitations, the differences in their paintings would result from only their subjective experience of the landscape. Se on the other hand, would go all out to produce paintings exactly like the landscape but, owing to the fact that everyone uses Si, the paintings would still have subjective qualities; it is just that extraverted sensors repress the subjective sensory experience in favor of the objective.

That is not to say that introverted sensing holds no value to Se; since despite the best efforts at observing the outer world objectively, one invariably comes up against the fact that one cannot sense the outer world without also sensing the effect that the world has upon oneself. Imagine that someone picks up a rock and says that the rock is hard. Se gives awareness of the rock, its shape, color, etc. It is introverted sensation, however, that believes the rock is hard because introverted sensation allows one to compare the sensory experience of the rock to things held in the past.

Of all the functions, Se is the least compatible with extraverted intuition. Se and extraverted intuition both perceive objectively; but where Se focuses on concrete, observable experiences, extraverted intuition focuses on possibilities. If it is Se that asks what is here right now, then extraverted intuition asks what if. Where Se is happy to take life as it comes, extraverted intuition feels a constant need to change the routine or plan.

That is because Se only focuses on the context given by the physical environment, but extraverted intuition considers many contexts, though far less thoroughly. As both Se and extraverted intuition are perceiving functions, neither is comfortable disagreeing outright, but if disagreement is offered, expect Se to discount possibilities that are unlikely to manifest in the observable outer world and extraverted intuition to offer possibilities meant to cause reconsideration.

As much as possible, Se aims to suppress its subjective aspect, which is introverted intuition. Extraverted sensors want to be as present in the moment as humanly possible; they crave hands-on experience. Taking the time to reflect on what their experiences mean to them, as is characteristic of introverted intuitives, keeps them from engaging with the world.

Se puts people directly in touch with the outer world and it is the filter through which people become aware of any concrete sensory information outside of themselves, whether Se is consciously used or not; introverted sensors say that the rock is hard only because they know the rock is there. Se unleashes force in the outer world to open doors, lift bags of groceries or shut the window. As a result, strong extraverted sensors are typically the best equipped to exert as much force as needed to get the job done, and not a bit more. This ability to apply the appropriate force even applies to less tangible things like extraverted sensors' ability to take concrete action at just the right moment, sometimes spoiling the best-laid plans.

Additionally, strong extraverted sensors generally have the finest motor skills among the types, owing to their high adaptation to the outer world. It should not be surprising, then, that many of the world's top athletes use extraverted sensing. Dominant extraverted sensors are quite adept at the social scene, not only because they are often aware of the latest styles, trends and gossip, but also because they catch even the smallest change in facial expression, tone of voice or body language. Se tends to have a very good memory for concrete details. Extraverted sensors are not likely to misplace their keys, trip over their own feet, or spill wine on their clothes because Se remains centered in the physical world and present moment.

While Se is highly attuned to the outside world, it is unable to do anything to tune into the inner world. It is only natural, then, that Se needs a partner to provide the self-awareness necessary to make sense of not only the subjective factor, but the objective factor, too.

Thus, all people who use Se also use introverted intuition since extraversion is opposed to introversion as is sensing to intuition.

Extraverted sensation depends on introverted intuition because without such intuition, it would be impossible to navigate the outer world successfully. Introverted intuition lends Se an inner perspective and a sense of purpose and meaning; without meaning, the objects of the physical world would be unassimilable because indistinct. Even a house cat knows that the sound of a can opening means that it is time for lunch. Similarly, when an extraverted sensor's alarm goes off, he might wake up, end his break, or step off the treadmill, but only because he has mapped a meaning onto the sensory experience.

Se might be incredibly aware of body language, but that awareness means nothing if the extraverted sensor is unable to determine what the body language means. While Se is great at getting immediate results in the outer world, the urge to act is the result of a seemingly irrepressible mental image–a kind of instinct, which is the word strong extraverted sensors often use to describe how introverted intuition feels to them.

Though some extraverted sensors might be reluctant to admit it, their superior ability to manipulate physical reality comes largely from Ni. Because Se is so attentive to the here and now, it is unable to predict even simple events on its own. Though Se might hear a growling dog and send adrenaline streaming through one's body, it is introverted intuition that knows it will be bitten if it gets any closer.

All people need Se, for without it, there would be zero awareness of the outside world. Se is of the utmost importance to the continued survival of humanity since it instantly spots any changes in the environment and acts on that information immediately. The fact that burgeoning humanity did not fall victim to the predator–prey dilemma, despite significant physical vulnerability, must largely be credited to Se's superior awareness of the physical world. Strong Se also endows one with the ability to find the tools in the immediate environment to complete a given task, relying on extensive improvisation if needed. Se would look at a mess in the kitchen, realize that there are no more cleaning supplies left and, then, search the kitchen cabinets for something that works, like apple cider vinegar.

Se tells a person in real time how far he can push a situation and still get the desired result. Se can gauge the limits so well not because of superior planning ability, but because of its natural oscillation between impulse and observation, like an old-fashioned metronome. For those reasons, Keirsey referred to strong extraverted sensors as tacticians par excellence.[19]

Introverted Intuition

Dominant: INFJ, INTJ
Auxiliary: ENFJ, ENTJ
Tertiary: ISFP, ISTP
Inferior: ESFP, ESTP

Introverted intuition, or Ni, is one of four introverted functions and one of four perceiving functions used by all people. Since Ni is oriented inwardly, it focuses subjectively on universals instead of particulars.

Like extraverted intuition, Ni gives its user insight into the background processes of the psyche. Unlike extraverted intuition, Ni does not aim to generate endless objective possibilities from a subjective data point. Ni, instead, allows its user to perceive the archetypal patterns at work in objective situations. Thus, strong introverted intuitives often perceive the psychic elements at work in any situation, as if perceiving past, present and future developments all at once. Ni aims to come to a singular and cohesive view of the situation and its meaning.

Imagine a brainstorming session. Extraverted intuition would be the function that takes a thesis and comes up with 20 different ways to explore it. Ni, on the contrary, would take 20 different ways to explore the topic and realize its thesis based on its exploration—exploration that largely takes place in the shadows of the unconscious.

Because Ni is oriented towards the subjective factor, its workings might seem bizarre to others. Extraverted intuition's advantage is that it is observable and related to collective understanding, though many feel that it is a bit quirky. Since introverted intuitives are tuning into unconscious contents, and unconscious contents defy explanation by their very nature, introverted intuitives often struggle to communicate the insights Ni gives them; in that regard, extraverted intuition is better off—as is to be expected from extraverted functions. The strange thing is, despite extraverted intuition's clear speed advantage, Ni often seems to arrive at the answer first because it does not travel to the answer but finds it within.

That is not to say that Ni has all the answers at its disposal, which is clearly not the case. Jung believed that Ni has a direct relation to the archetypes. "[The archetype] undoubtedly does express unconscious contents, but not the whole of them, only those that are momentarily constellated."[20] Thus, before an answer can become conscious to Ni, its user needs empirical contents that are, at least, somewhat conscious and that correspond to the insight that Ni is attempting to share with its user. For example, this function will not give a person an intelligible insight into a cure for cancer if the person does not know enough about the disease, the human body and medicine.

Of all the cognitive functions, Ni is the least compatible with introverted sensing. Both functions allow one to perceive one's inner world subjectively, but each function focuses on content that is entirely different. Ni tunes into the background processes of the psyche; introverted sensation peers into the background processes of sensory experience. Strong introverted intuition, unfortunately, looks on introverted sensing as a bit shallow and stuck in the past, and introverted intuitives will only focus on introverted sensing when their bodies cry out for attention.

That is largely because Ni is the most abstract cognitive function in that it operates largely outside of conscious awareness, while introverted sensing is the most practical introverted function in that it is a subjective map of objective sensory experience. As a result, introverted sensing is highly attuned to the realities of daily life, while Ni is focused on hidden meanings and cohesion.

Extraverted sensation is Ni's objective aspect, and Ni aims to suppress its influence as much as possible in order to reach Ni's goal: to give its users an all-encompassing sense of subjective meaning regarding the objective world and their experience of it.

Strong Ni is associated with the ability to perceive hidden relationships between phenomena, and it is the best function at getting a peak at what is going on behind the curtain. Ni is nothing like the feeling and thinking functions in bringing to light those things that appear to be hidden because Ni does not analyze logically to find the truth. Instead, Ni takes in voluminous data, unconsciously finds the patterns and underlying meanings, and when the introverted intuitive is relaxed, a mental image appears that unites all the disparate aspects in a way that elucidates underlying causation.

Thus, coherence plays just as important a role for the introverted intuitive as it does for the judging types. However, introverted intuitives will not rely on thought or feeling to assess coherence, but will compare incoming information against their internal, archetypal map of the world. Ni will deem ideas that fit the map to be coherent or worthwhile, even if there is a degree of contradiction. Unlike judging functions, Ni does not necessarily view contradiction as indicative of an irredeemable flaw in an idea or argument because it instinctively realizes that the contradiction could be the result of an incomplete understanding of the underlying laws of nature. Strong introverted intuitives can identify with a viewpoint that they do not truly hold and have learned from an early age that what is right or wrong, true or false, has a way of changing depending on how one looks at the matter or who is looking. Accordingly, dominant introverted intuitives typically look for reasons why something could be true, whereas people who rely more on a judging function typically look to dismiss contradictory information immediately. Paired with strong extraverted judgment, Ni has an enormous advantage because it can find treasures that others abandoned. On the other hand, introverted intuitives with poor extraverted judgment appear to be profoundly out of touch with the real world because they fail to test their intuitive insights against reality.

While Ni is great at giving its users insight into their own minds and their place in the world, it does a comparatively poor job making them aware of the realities of daily life. It follows, then, that Ni needs a counterpart to provide the concrete perceptions onto which Ni maps subjective meaning.

Anyone who uses introverted intuition must also utilize extraverted sensation since introversion is opposed to extraversion, as is intuition to sensation.

Without extraverted sensation, Ni would be unable to make unconscious, archetypal contents conscious. Since archetypes are forms without content, it is only when extraverted sensing fills those forms with content that they are activated and become available for Ni to work its magic. Ni, more than any other function, is associated with the ability to predict the future accurately. Extraverted sensation is the *sine qua non* without which Ni's workings would bear no relation to tangible reality.

Strong introverted intuitives are often credited for having the best imaginative abilities of all types; and it is obvious that in the creation of anything, imagination is of the utmost importance because it is imagination that allows one to see what is unseen. Since Ni is introverted and deals with potentialities, not realities, Ni depends on extraverted sensation to make Ni's dream tangible. This applies to creations as concrete as original inventions, or to more subtle pursuits like implementing the most effective strategy or getting the most people to give to charity.

Though some introverted intuitives might think otherwise, even the most carefully laid plans and ideas run into unexpected difficulties when it comes time for implementation. Strong Ni typically comes prepared with contingency plans because introverted intuitives are not as comfortable taking immediate action as strong extraverted sensors. Thus, well-integrated extraverted sensation is essential to allowing introverted intuitives not only to spot problems in real time, but also to take immediate action to remedy any issues.

Ni is essential to the world because Ni is the only function that allows one to form any realization regarding one's inner psychic nature. Ni is the function that allows a person to think of herself from a third-person perspective. Strong introverted intuitives tend to have superior self-awareness as a result; and that applies even more to INTJ and INFJ because they not only utilize introverted intuition as their dominant function, but also rely on their tertiary introverted judgment, which lends a high-degree of self-knowledge. Such people are aware not only of their motivations, but also of the psychic causes for those motivations.

It is impossible to imagine living in the observable world without an ability to relate to it. Though the contents of observable reality would continue to exist, they would not continue existing to the absent observer. Yet in another sense, there are no smells, sounds, tastes, sights or things to touch without someone to sense them; and the link between the objects of sensory experience and the one who senses them describes a necessary relationship, for distinguishing oneself from an object requires that subject and object hold distinct meanings.

Extraverted sensation engages directly with the real world, but Ni allows one to find the meaning that underlies one's experience of life.

Introverted Sensation-Extraverted Intuition Axis

Within the Si-Ne, or introverted sensation-extraverted intuition dichotomy, are some who prefer Si to Ne and others who prefer Ne to Si.

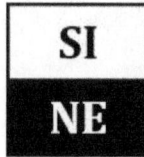

SI
NE

Introverted sensation and extraverted intuition are always opposed to each other, showing that each function is part of a larger process.

People who use the Si-Ne perception dichotomy perceive physical reality at an individual level, somewhat abstracted from direct sensory experience; their sensory experience lies within. On the other hand, Si-Ne types find meaning and possibilities outside of them.

To Si-Ne types, physical experience is open to debate since everyone assimilates sense experience individually, but there is no dispute about what an experience means to the world.

That is because Ne assimilates to the object, thereby minimizing one's individual sense of meaning in favor of maximizing the collective's. In those who prefer Ne to Si, this point of view is decisive and weds these people to a deeply shared yet flexible experience of meaning.

In those who prefer Si to Ne, one finds the opposite tendency. This is because Si relates objective meaning to the subject in a cohesive way: through one's body. Thus, a strong Si user might identify a movie's climax by noticing when she felt the most tension in her body and when that tension was released.

Si could not link subjective experience to outer possibilities unless it had some awareness of the possibilities, so Ne is essential to Si's operations.

Ne would not truly be aware of objective possibilities if it had no idea how those possibilities impact physical experience, so Si is fundamental to Ne. For instance, many poisonous toads successfully sport exotic colors to make predators aware of their toxicity, an elementary example of the relationship between Ne and Si. No matter what the predator's physical perception of the exotic colors might be, the colors have a collective meaning that is instinctually understood. As is the case with any information, this same predator-prey experience could be viewed through a Se-Ni prism.

People who prefer to use this dichotomy are quite open to new possibilities and ideas, especially when Ne is preferred to Si; but Si-Ne types tend to demonstrate greater caution than their Se-Ni counterparts in maintaining physical equilibrium, and Si-Ne types display this caution by staying in close connection with their database of life experience. This tendency is, of course, magnified in those who prefer Si to Ne.

Si-Ne outwardly appears to be more scattered and distracted than Se-Ni because Si-Ne is always focused, at least in part, on objective possibilities, not objective reality. Inwardly, the situation is reversed; because Si-Ne types' inner worlds always have an eye toward the past and their histories, they tend to be more structured and focused inwardly.

Compared to Se-Ni types, Si-Ne types demonstrate greater ease with communication because the meaning and possibilities they seek to communicate are shared by everybody.

Introverted Sensing

Dominant: ISFJ, ISTJ
Auxiliary: ESFJ, ESTJ
Tertiary: INFP, INTP
Inferior: ENFP, ENTP

Introverted sensation, or Si, is one of four introverted cognitive functions and one of four perceiving functions common to all. Since Si is oriented to the inner world, it subjectively focuses on universals.

Like extraverted sensation, Si allows its user to become aware of the world through the senses. Unlike extraverted sensation, Si is not interested in perceiving every nuance of an object's outer appearance; instead, it perceives what the object is like to the subject, relative to experience. In practice, that means Se is highly aware of the action occurring in the immediate environment, while Si is attentive to how the environment affects the subject. Introverted sensors are typically the most aware of how their bodies are feeling, usually having built an extensive catalog of how certain experiences affect their internal sense of well-being. Extraverted sensors are, of course, aware of their bodies, but the stimulus of the outside world is what really draws their attention. As a result, extraverted sensation prefers action and style, while Si prefers comfort and stability.

Introverted sensors have an internal map of sensory experience that they use to navigate the world. Imagine eating pasta for dinner. An introverted sensor might say the sauce was tangy or spicy. However, those are not objective, measurable qualities in and of themselves; i.e., tanginess and spiciness can only be measured in terms of something else, like the amount of pepper or tomato paste used. Thus, terms like spicy or tangy are not indicative of extraverted sensation. Enter Si's internal map. Si compares the pasta to everything previously eaten using its map, and it is this relationship between the past and present that comes to an introverted sensor's conscious mind.

Because Si is the vehicle that carries past sensory experience, strong Si users tend to be more prepared for the future than extraverted sensors because Si users scour their internal map for similar situations and quickly move to apply what has worked before. The tradeoff is that Si is not nearly as capable of handling unpredictable changes in the environment, which extraverted sensing finds invigorating.

All of this means that while extraverted sensation welcomes risks, accepts change and embraces opportunities for improvisation, Si likes to take a more conservative method, sticking to tried-and-true approaches, and doing everything in its power to avoid unnecessary gambles. Why should the things that have always worked change?

Of all the cognitive functions, Si is the least compatible with introverted intuition. Even though both functions form inner frameworks for understanding the world, those frameworks could hardly be more different in their substance. Si maps sensory experience, introverted intuition maps psychic experience. As a result, Si feels a strong link to the past, whereas introverted intuition peers into the future. It is no wonder, then, that introverted sensors tend to feel that introverted intuitives not only make life pointlessly complicated, but also have little evidence on which to base their approach.

To an outside observer, Si might very well seem like the most practical of the introverted functions because of its conventional approach to life. Introverted sensors, therefore, value routine, stability and authority. Introverted intuition, with its highly abstract nature, could not care less about tradition.

As much as possible, Si strives to suppress its objective aspect, extraverted intuition, in order to fulfill its goal: to perceive the effects that sensory experience has upon the subject. In doing so, Si naturally conserves memory of the effects, and seems to perpetuate those things and activities that have previously brought comfort, happiness or success.

When Si is in the dominant or auxiliary positions, one finds people with incredible memories. Not only will these people have incredible factual recall, they will also remember tastes and smells with accuracy. Strong introverted sensors can often remember important events in their lives with photographic exactness. For example, introverted sensors are likely to remember the tiniest details from their wedding days, even twenty years later. Not only will introverted sensors remember everything about their dresses, where they purchased their attire and how well the dresses fit, they will also remember how the gowns' fabric felt on their skin, or the way their fathers clutched their hands as they walked down the aisle, or the exact words of their vows. They are unlikely to forget important dates like anniversaries and birthdays, and they will definitely be prepared to honor those dates in traditional ways.

To Si, authority is something to be esteemed, whether at home, at school or at work; rules are made to be followed, not worked around; cash is to be saved, not thrown away on frivolous shopping sprees.

Introverted sensing's focus on conservation means that Si loathes one word: change. Imagine a gentleman who has gone to the same coffee house every morning for two years. The barista made his latte every day for over a year now, but the barista just started a new job. Today, it is someone new. An introverted sensor would remember how long it took the last barista to learn the way he likes his drink, and now he believes he will have to live through weeks of disappointing lattes before the new barista catches on.

Anyone who uses introverted sensation also uses extraverted intuition because introversion is opposed to extraversion, as is sensation to intuition.

Without extraverted intuition, introverted sensors would be powerless to use Si's vast storehouse of data to choose the best course of action because it is extraverted intuition that is able to see how the present situation is objectively like the past. Extraverted intuition is Si's needed creative aspect. Si's penchant for maintaining what has come before means that it is prone to stagnation. Just as Si keeps extraverted intuition from reaching a state of complete sublimation, extraverted intuition protects Si from paralysis. Extraverted intuition lends Si a desire to make new friends, learn new hobbies, try new recipes or restaurants, and form new memories. Si's preference for learning from experience would be untenable if extraverted intuition were not there to give Si's experience a sense of meaning, context and possibilities for exploration.

Of all the cognitive functions, Si's worldview does the best job of eliminating risk. Si's reliance on tested ways of doing things produces consistent results, even if some might find it a bit stale. Strong introverted sensors consistently save their money, work diligently to earn promotions at work, adhere to rules and procedures, and support their communities, whether at church, through volunteer work or by donating to charity. Aversion to risk leads strong introverted sensors to demand building inspections, vaccinations or comprehensive evacuation plans. Si would rather take the time to check the details than live with the possibility of unforeseen disappointment.

"To expect the unexpected shows a thoroughly modern intellect," said Oscar Wilde, and there is little doubt that Si hates anything more than being unprepared for the unexpected. Though some introverted sensors might not want to hear it, the past, while instructive, can never predict the future. Si cannot deal with the unexpected traffic jam on the preferred route to work; it cannot propose a viable way to handle a unique and unanticipated challenge. If Si lacks the experiences needed to help it cope with surprises, it must rely on extraverted intuition to provide further possibilities. Unfortunately, strong Si-types most often use extraverted intuition to see what will go wrong instead of what could go right.

Si is critical to humanity, and everyone uses it. Si records one's experiences, views, insights, ideas and personal sense of history. Without Si, activities like learning to read, write or do math would be impossible since the ability to remember is a crucial aspect of learning. The word that comes closest to describing what Si does is memory. Much like extraverted sensation, Si is of central importance to humanity's continued survival. Si's focus on maintaining a natural balance between an individual's sense of the world and the world itself helped ensure that poisonous mushrooms did not wipe out whole tribes, that villages stored enough supplies to survive the winter, and that hunters increased their effectiveness by recognizing animal tracks.

Extraverted Intuition

Dominant: ENFP, ENTP
Auxiliary: INFP, INTP
Tertiary: ESFJ, ESTJ
Inferior: ISFJ, ISTJ

Extraverted intuition, or Ne, is one of four extraverted cognitive functions and one of four perceiving functions used by all. Because Ne is oriented to the outer world, it objectively focuses on particulars.

Like introverted intuition, Ne allows its user to find meaning in the world. Unlike introverted intuition, Ne is not interested in an all-encompassing sense of meaning; that would be far too static a framework. Instead, Ne focuses on generating numerous possibilities from a subjective data point. Where Ni eliminates possibilities based on the likelihood of those possibilities playing out in the real world, Ne finds that approach too restrictive. Ne prefers to entertain all possibilities no matter how absurd they seem on the surface, and when dominant extraverted intuitives need to draw conclusions, they must rely on their introverted judgment to discard implausible possibilities.

Imagine a family camping in the woods holding flashlights to get around on a dark night. Extraverted intuition is the light spreading out from a flashlight; introverted intuition would see the diffused light and follow it back to its source.

Since Ne tunes into objective meanings, its use does not strike others as strange; that is not the case for introverted intuition. However, Ne's desire to ask what if to so many of life's situations can wear other people out because it seems that

Ne is unable to accept life as it is. Since Ne is extraverted and able to generate possibilities with incredible speed, dominant extraverted intuitives typically have the greatest verbal fluency of all the types; they are never stumped for a credible answer to even the most challenging questions. It is no surprise then, that so many TV reporters and anchors use Ne. On the other hand, introverted intuition lacks that fluency in the outer world because it is introverted and concerned not with infinite possibilities, but with a unified sense of meaning.

Since Ni works with psychic universals, there is a strange way in which it holds all points of view at once, but never fully identifies with those views. Ne, however, hates to hold onto anything for too long. Instead of holding multiple potential points of view at one time, Ne works through the possibilities in a sequential fashion, moving from the possibilities that are most exciting to those that are most bland. Once Ne has a handle on the potentials inherent in the situation, it might consider the relationships between all the possibilities.

Among the cognitive functions, Ne is least compatible with extraverted sensing. That is because both functions perceive objective reality, but both work with different content. Extraverted sensation strives to reproduce faithfully the outer world for its user, focusing on tangible reality. Ne seeks to find every option related to the objective situation. Because possibilities are intangible, it is clear that Ne deals with abstractions. Extraverted intuition and extraverted sensation are similar in that once the objective situation is experienced to its fullest, both functions are ready to move on.

In the same way that extraverted sensing is the instrument by which everyone not only perceives physical reality, but also creates, shapes and alters it, Ne aims to shape and refine objective ideas and meanings.

Introverted sensation is Ne's subjective aspect, and as far as possible, Ne works to suppress introverted sensation to fulfill Ne's purpose, which is to bring change by communicating to the world that there is more to be considered.

Strong Ne is generally associated with an ability to see the potential in any situation, person or object. Thus, extraverted intuitives tend to be the most entrepreneurial types, improvising in any way needed to get hold of the prospects sought. As is the case with all the extraverted functions, Ne characteristically adjusts to the outside world. But unlike extraverted feeling and extraverted thinking, Ne does not adjust for the sake of making another feel welcome or for efficiency's sake. Rather, Ne adjusts itself according to objective meaning, sometimes causing strong extraverted intuitives to contort themselves in the most uncomfortable ways just to be prepared to exploit a possibility that might, or might not, manifest in the outer world. Extraverted intuitives who have sufficiently strengthened their introverted judgment tend to have healthy boundaries about how much they will bend for the world, and their gambles pay off more often than not. Extraverted intuitives with weak introverted judgment, however, might end up forsaking themselves in pursuit of what might be.

While Ne gives its user incredible potential to change the world, it does a relatively poor job of giving the extraverted intuitive the sense of steadiness, both physical and mental, to see change through to the end. Accordingly, Ne needs a stable foundation on which it can build its house of potentialities.

Anyone who uses extraverted intuition must also use introverted sensation because extraversion is opposed to introversion, as is intuition to sensing.

Without introverted sensation, Ne could not access the subjective sensory data from which it is able to derive countless possibilities. If extraverted sensation were tasked with describing a glass of water, for example, it would study it and give concrete descriptions of the glass's size, fullness and shape. Ne, however, would use introverted sensing and come up with subjective data points, sensing that the glass of water is cold, which is not a description of the glass of water in and of itself, rather a description of the glass of water as it appears to introverted sensing. Something can only be cold in relation to something that is hot. That sensory comparison is not under the purview of extraverted sensing, but introverted sensing. From the data point of cold, Ne would generate possibilities that objectively relate to a cold glass of water. For example, Ne-users might say that the glass of water reminds them of a refreshing beverage on a hot summer day, or a lake whose surface has frozen over. Though none of those possibilities are physically present, they all bear relation to the glass of water that most people could readily explain.

Strong extraverted intuitives generally do the best brainstorming of all the types because they quickly spot how one thing relates to another. Ne is unlike any other function in that it will not discard data simply because it seems unlikely to lead anywhere or work out as expected. Even introverted intuition chooses to gloss over the implausible and, of course, people cannot use their five senses to become aware of something that is impossible, for its very impossibility means that there is nothing to be sensed; last, the ability to quickly discard information is essential to all judging functions.

Though some extraverted intuitives might not want to admit it, not every possibility can become reality. In some cases, one possibility coming into reality precludes another. The light in the next room is either on or off, for example. Before one enters the room, the light being on or off are both real possibilities; but once the room is entered, only one possibility can be a concrete reality. Introverted sensation is, thus, indispensable to Ne since introverted sensation provides the data points to which Ne must orient itself; otherwise, Ne would skid off the rails in its quest for change.

Ne is essential to the world and everyone uses it to varying degrees because it is the function most associated with objective transformation. Without Ne, the world would be in danger of inertia. Introverted intuitives might have the best imaginations, but without extraverted intuitives' ability to observe, remain open to and seize opportunities for change, the world would probably still be working with Newtonian physics and riding horses instead of driving cars.

It is difficult to envision a world in which objective possibilities do not exist. Failure could not become success; the student could not become the teacher; the employee could never become the employer; disease could never become health. The 13 original colonies never could have become the most powerful country the world has seen. Therefore, Ne's ability to envision potential outcomes and communicate the possibilities to others improves life for everyone.

Judgment

Introverted Feeling-Extraverted Thinking Axis

People who consciously use the Fi-Te, or introverted feeling-extraverted thinking dichotomy, believe that thought belongs to the group while feelings belong to the individual.

FI

TE

Introverted feeling and extraverted thinking are always opposed to each other, showing that each function is part of a larger process.

To Fi-Te types, common sense manifests as awareness that there are effective and ineffective ways to reach the goal; that rules, guidelines and procedures are there to be followed. At the same time, these types are quite willing to allow all to hold and display their unique values and emotions, even if it results in a bit of social discomfort. Accordingly, Fi-Te types are open to criticism about efficiency, productivity and concrete results, but fiercely maintain their right to feel as they please.

Fi-Te types are typically focused on structuring the world in logical ways because by doing so, they provide the space needed not only to work out their own ethics and emotions, but to ensure that their individual principles are not overrun by mob values.

Some who use the Fi-Te dichotomy are more skilled with Fi, the others with Te.

When Fi is ascendant (i.e., when Fi is more conscious than Te), the individual is deeply attuned to her individual dreams, hopes and aspirations. People who are more skilled with Fi than Te give valuable assistance by insisting that regulations and policies do not take on an importance greater than that of the people who those systems are meant to serve.

When Te is ascendant, the individual is deeply attuned to collective ideas regarding law, order and empirical validation. Thus, people who are more skilled with Te than Fi offer an important service. Since Te is willing to forgo a bit of authenticity for the sake of effectiveness and it is unperturbed from directly offering its point of view, strong extraverted thinkers provide the space for strong Fi-types to hold their individuality.

When one digs deeply enough, one finds that at the heart of Te's assumptions are value judgments: Te instinctively values standardization, rules, structure and efficiency, even though Te will decide for itself what each of these values looks like in the outer world.

At the heart of Fi-types' value of authenticity is deep factual knowledge of what has happened when they have forsaken themselves for others. Fi makes it possible to structure the outer world in accordance with one's individual values and that is necessary since, in many cases, logic is useless. Red cars are not more factual or effective than blue cars, yet some people prefer one color to the other. Strong Fi-types are acutely aware of the mechanisms behind such judgments.

Introverted Feeling

Dominant: ISFP, INFP
Auxiliary: ESFP, ENFP
Tertiary: ISTJ, INTJ
Inferior: ESTJ, ENTJ

Introverted feeling, or Fi, is one of four introverted functions, and one of four judging functions. Since this function is oriented to the inner world, introverted feelers are chiefly concerned with universal, subjective matters.

Like extraverted feeling, Fi forms and refines value judgments about what is moral or immoral, tasteful or tasteless, authentic or inauthentic, and right or wrong. Unlike extraverted feeling, Fi does not aim to create agreement in the outer world, but the inner. Introverted feelers rely on their inner wisdom to make value judgments, whereas extraverted feelers derive their values from the worlds of family, community and society. Authenticity is, perhaps, the best word to describe Fi's role in life.

Where extraverted feeling is typically concerned with forging and maintaining harmony between people, Fi is most concerned with faithfulness to self.

Another difference between Fi and extraverted feeling comes from the fact that extraverted feelers are more than happy to be untrue to self for the sake of others. Because the extraverted feeler's values are collectively held, extraverted feelers will not be overly concerned with forming value judgments that are not in accord with their personal feelings. Introverted feelers, on the other hand, hate to behave in ways in discord with their own values, even if that behavior will help others. If an introverted feeler sacrifices for anybody, it is either because she has a deep moral conviction on the matter or a strong personal connection to the person she is helping.

It is not that Fi places little value on the things and ideas that tie people together. Rather, because it has learned from experience that there is no society without individuals, and since society's value judgments are simply products of a harmonious intertwining of individual value judgments, Fi is more than happy to refine its own ideas rather than force them on others. Of all the cognitive functions, it is easily the most concerned with sincerity, which extraverted feeling is sometimes willing to abandon.

Fi is least compatible with introverted thinking because both functions seek to structure the inner world, but with conflicting aims and ideas regarding what is most important. Because of the inward orientation of both functions, introverted feelers and thinkers rarely experience conflict with each other in the outer world; but internally, these types have little regard for each other's approach to life.

Fi aims to structure the inner world by what its users feel is most important, most pleasing and most true to self. Introverted thinking structures the inner world according to frameworks derived from the rules of deductive logic. Fi depends on the human element to do its job. On the other hand, introverted thinking aims to remove value judgments from its calculus.

As much as possible, Fi strives to suppress its objective aspect, extraverted thinking, so that it can fulfill its agenda: to make decisions that are faithful to its users' values.

Fi is usually earnest because it hates to be treated in manners that do not resonate with its truth. Earnestness is why many perceive strong introverted feelers to be the best listeners of all the types; introverted feelers are in touch with their own individuality, so they have no qualms about allowing others to express their uniqueness. It might seem that extraverted feelers would be better listeners but owing to their focus on applying values to the outer world, they typically believe there is an appropriate way to feel and behave. As a result, the extraverted feeler struggles to listen with an open mind. That said, Fi is far less likely than extraverted feeling to change its views because Fi's values are inherently individual.

Fi is reflective, and introverted feelers expect their individuality to be respected; it is otherwise impossible to earn their trust. Fi will not allow itself to be forced into acting in any way contrary to itself, and introverted feelers do not appreciate attempts to make them display emotions they do not genuinely feel. Introverted feelers typically prefer that group interactions allow all to express their true feelings and views, rather than interactions in which group harmony is more important than faithfulness to self, which is often the case with extraverted feeling.

While introverted feelers are great at understanding what is important to themselves, Fi cannot clarify or resolve all of life's issues alone. Consequently, this function needs a counterpart not only to judge matters of an impersonal nature, but also to apply its personal judgments to the outer world.

Anyone who uses introverted feeling must also utilize extraverted thinking since introversion is opposed to extraversion, as feeling is to thinking.

Though Fi is critical to allowing people to get in touch with their inner natures, it is not equipped to meet the challenges of the outside world. Without some way to understand and manipulate tangible reality, Fi would be unable to uphold or defend those values that make everyone unique; the world would suffer too since strong introverted feelers are the best at ensuring fairness and integrity are at the core of impersonal systems.

Fi is unable to design or implement a system in physical reality, for example. To structure the world around them, introverted feelers must rely on their extraverted thinking. Strong Fi is often associated with efforts to structure the world in ways not necessarily aimed at peak efficiency, as would be seen in someone favors extraverted thinking over Fi, but instead in a manner meant to align with its values, ideas and emotions. Introverted feelers are less likely to pick a college major with job prospects and salary as the primary motivators than they are to pick a major based on the subjects about which they are most passionate.

Some introverted feelers might not like to hear it, but extraverted thinking is the force that fuels Fi. It is impossible to value something without knowing what it is, and such knowledge is the domain of the thinking function. Since Fi judges internally, extraverted thinking provides the real-world facts, standards and criteria by which Fi expresses violations of its values to the outer world, when it bothers to express the violations at all.

The world would not be the same without this function, and every person makes some use of it since Fi evaluates, weighs, resolves and orders one's personal feelings about the environment, other people and oneself. Without this brand of feeling, the relationship between mother and child would not hold its archetypal potency. The personal bond between parent and child, or between siblings, friends, or spouses is not a value that is derived outwardly because personal bonds emerge out of the core of one's being. Similarly, personal feelings of anger, joy, disappointment or disillusionment are expressions of an individual's inner values.

Lacking introverted feeling, there could be no individual value judgments. It would be impossible to determine what to eat for dinner, the preferred vacation spot or what movie to see. Because extraverted feelers often have a hard time getting in touch with their own feelings, they often need to rely on sounding things out to resolve such dilemmas. Fi is also the tool that allows one to feel genuine empathy for others because it is the only cognitive function that allows one to put oneself in another's situation and feel at a deep, internal level what the other's experience is like. Fi is not so great at displaying the level of warmth and sympathy characteristic of extraverted feeling, and it is not uncommon to hear extraverted feelers describe Fi as cold or numb as a result.

People's feelings regarding their self-esteem come from an internal valuation. An individual's sense of adequacy, attractiveness and desirability are personally held views, even if others helped to form the views.

Extraverted Thinking

Dominant: ESTJ, ENTJ
Auxiliary: ISTJ, INTJ
Tertiary: ESFP, ENFP
Inferior: ISFP, INFP

Extraverted thinking, or Te, is one of four extraverted functions and one of four judging functions that all people use. Owing to its outwardly oriented nature, it is concerned with particular, objective data.

Like introverted thinking, Te is chiefly concerned with distinctions between what is or what is not, what is correct or incorrect, and what is true or false. Unlike introverted thinking, Te does not gauge an idea's validity by means of deductive reasoning or the formal rules of logic, which are archetypal. Instead, Te prefers inductive reasoning, meaning it relies on facts, examples and proven data to provide empirical support. Indeed, empirical is the word that best describes Te.

Where introverted thinking typically has more of a philosophical bent on seeking truth, Te's insistence on measurable results favors a scientific approach.

Another distinction between Te and introverted thought comes from the fact that introverted thinkers' primary goal is to understand a topic completely; strong Ti-types care little about how useful their understanding will be in the outer world. Te is only interested in understanding something insofar as its understanding facilitates achieving a certain end. For example, an introverted thinker might begin studying psychology only because she wants to understand herself better. An extraverted thinker, on the contrary, would have a goal in mind, like improving relations with his employees or his public image.

That is not to say that Te has no regard for logically consistent arguments as measures of truth. However, because this function is so concerned with effectiveness, extraverted thinkers are likely to remember times when a logically valid argument proved to be wrong because it overlooked key factors relevant to implementation in the world. Speaking of memory, extraverted thinkers tend to have remarkable memory of factual data or systems, which only introverted sensing surpasses. Extraverted thinkers' strong memory in no way applies to their interpersonal relations, however.

Of all the cognitive functions, Te is the least compatible with extraverted feeling because both aim to structure the world, but with conflicting aims and ideas regarding what is most important. Unfortunately, strong extraverted thinkers tend to find extraverted feeling unnatural, almost repulsive, and they will only rely on it when it serves their agenda.

That is because Te lends structure and guidelines for effectiveness to a person's outer life, much like extraverted feeling. However, where extraverted feeling is chiefly concerned with the principles and values that govern effective human interaction, Te is more concerned with effective systems, rules and laws, i.e., the impersonal world.

As far as possible, Te aims to suppress its subjective aspect, introverted feeling, so that it can fulfill its aim: to arrive at unbiased, fact-based determinations of truth for which there is broad agreement.

People who consciously use Te tend to have a natural air of authority and competence, owing to their focus on achieving goals. That laser focus means that extraverted thinkers are naturally decisive—so decisive in fact, that they often seem incredibly stubborn. While there are good reasons that extraverted thinkers are viewed as stubborn, those reasons miss the point that most extraverted thinkers are more than willing to change their minds and approaches if someone politely shows empirical reasons for why the extraverted thinkers are wrong. Appeals to values, or even deductive logic, are unlikely to result in extraverted thinkers reconsidering their position if they believe they have stronger factual support. Nevertheless, extraverted thinkers are generally much more willing to alter their views on a matter than those who prefer introverted judgment, despite the respective tones in delivering their ideas.

Te is action-oriented; extraverted thinkers expect to see results yesterday and not a moment later. Te does not merely like efficiency. Te demands it. As a result, extraverted thinkers have little tolerance for those who behave unproductively, and because Te is most concerned with achieving desired results in the outer world, extraverted thinkers can be quite blunt or condescending to those who they feel are slacking. Since, to its users, this function tends to feel like common sense, extraverted thinkers typically will not feel bad about correcting, even harshly, those who violate their common-sense law: efficiency.

While Te is great at resolving impersonal problems, some of life's problems and joys are decidedly personal because people do not live life apart from themselves or others. Thus, Te needs a counterpart to form value judgments and an understanding about the complexities of human nature.

Anyone who uses extraverted thinking necessarily utilizes introverted feeling since extraversion is opposed to introversion, as is thinking to feeling.

There are endless issues of an impersonal nature to consider in the outer world, so without some inner compass, extraverted thinkers would be unable to hone in on any particular goal. The ability of strong extraverted thinkers to focus on a single goal is a significant key to their success, and their high valuation of focus provides the fuel for their drive.

Te is incapable of deciding what is fair or unfair because it is necessarily true that, in any case, logical arguments exist for either side. Consequently, Te relies on introverted feeling to form such judgments. Strong extraverted thinkers will not concern themselves directly with how others feel, unless a strong personal bond exists. Instead, strong extraverted thinkers tend to ask themselves questions like, "How would I feel if it were me who were being affected by this judgment?" "Would I think this outcome is good if the shoe were on the other foot?" After such reflection, extraverted thinkers will have no qualms about quickly applying their value judgments to the outer world.

Though some extraverted thinkers might hate to admit it, hobbies are symptoms of value judgments as well. Te could dig into innumerable interests or activities. The force that makes extraverted thinkers feel that one hobby is worth pursuing more than another is introverted feeling. It is the force that helps strong extraverted thinkers stick with their interests until they show some degree of competence because extraverted thinkers value competence.

Te is essential to the world and all people use it because this function makes, understands and enforces rules, regulations, policies, procedures and laws. Te is the applier of systems. Whenever people drive cars, they are operating in Te world; people stop at the red lights and go at the green lights, not because green logically means go or red logically means stop, but because assigning the colors those meanings is key to the traffic system. Similarly, driving on the right side of the road is not logical per se; people drive on the left side of the road in other countries. However, it is necessary that a coherent system governs life on the road.

Imagine if people could drive cars according to their value judgments, or according to their personal thoughts regarding logical validity. One could easily foresee a chaotic scene. That is where another aspect of Te comes in: standardization. Te does not care if someone is rich or poor; each person needs to follow the rules, and should one fail to do so, one will face the appropriate consequences. College entrance exams are another example of a Te system; doing well on the tests does not necessarily make a person smart in the ways that matter, neither does doing poorly mean one is dumb. It is necessary, however, that there is a standardized way to assess students' readiness for college admittance since the other variables are either difficult or impossible to standardize. To an extraverted thinker, standardization is key to effective comparison, but others sometimes feel that Te, more so than any other function, ignores the human element.

Te is essential to effective management, whether its use feels natural or not. People with strong extraverted thinking are the most comfortable of all types giving direct orders, so it is common to find them in positions with executive authority. Strong extraverted thinkers have no problem telling it like it is. If Te is mixed with good introverted feeling, extraverted thinkers can often state their viewpoints without doing lasting damage to their relationships. Unfortunately, properly integrated introverted feeling is a rarity among strong extraverted thinkers and their Te sometimes leaves wounds that can be difficult to heal.

Extraverted Feeling-Introverted Thinking Axis

People who consciously use the Fe-Ti, or extraverted feeling-introverted thinking dichotomy, believe that feelings belong to the group while thought belongs to the individual.

FE
TI

Extraverted feeling and introverted thinking are always opposed to each other, showing that each function is part of a larger process.

To Fe-Ti types, common sense manifests as a mindfulness that there are appropriate feelings, values and emotions, that all people have social roles that must be played. On the other hand, Fe-Ti types tune into their individuality through their conclusions and logical frameworks, and they allow everyone else to do the same, even if it results in some factual ambiguity. Accordingly, these types are quite open to criticisms about their values or beliefs but will fight fiercely for their right to think as they see fit.

Fe-Ti types are typically focused on maintaining an atmosphere of peace and harmony because by doing so, they provide the space not only needed for others to think and believe as each deems appropriate, but also for all to pursue their fullest understanding of the world and themselves.

Some who use the Fe-Ti dichotomy consciously are more skilled with Fe, while the others are better with Ti.

When Fe is ascendant, the individual is deeply attuned to collective values and cultural norms. Thus, strong Fe-types provide Ti-types a crucial service since Fe is willing to forgo a degree of logical accuracy for the sake of smooth, well-lubricated communications.

When Ti is ascendant, the individual is aware of her individual ideas about logical structure and validity. Strong Ti-types return Fe-types' favor by reminding them that smooth social interactions are facilitated by a clear sense of the rules that govern effective communication.

When one digs deeply enough, one finds that at the heart of Ti's efforts are underlying value judgments: Ti instinctively values logical consistency, truth, accuracy and precision, even though Ti will decide for itself how each of these values applies to the inner world.

At the heart of Fe's value of harmonious interaction are the logical rules that make such interactions possible. For example, a strong Fe-type is likely to conclude that it is inappropriate to discuss politics at Thanksgiving dinner. When one considers the matter, however, it is hard to miss all the logical assumptions that go into such an idea: political discussions are divisive, Thanksgiving dinners are about bringing people together, not dividing them; thoughts and activities that are divisive are inappropriate.

Extraverted Feeling

Dominant: ESFJ, ENFJ
Auxiliary: ISFJ, INFJ
Tertiary: ESTP, ENTP
Inferior: ISTP, INTP

Extraverted feeling, or Fe, is one of four extraverted functions, and one of four judging functions. Because Fe is concerned with the outer world, extraverted feelers like to deal with particular value judgments.

Like introverted feeling, Fe focuses on values, emotions and harmony. Unlike introverted feeling, Fe is not concerned with individual authenticity and a sense of inner congruence, but with forging accord and consensus between individuals. Because Fe is little concerned with its own opinions and values, strong introverted feelers tend to believe that extraverted feelers are phony. On the other hand, extraverted feelers believe that introverted feelers' concern with their own opinions seems selfish. Introverted feelers should remember that Fe wants to establish positive feelings between individuals, and as long as Fe is working to do so, it is just as true to itself as introverted feeling.

Some of the conflict between introverted and extraverted feeling comes from the fact that Fe establishes values according to objective standards. As a result, strong extraverted feelers tend to take on the morals and ideals of their families, friends and communities. Strong extraverted feelers also believe, often unconsciously, that values are context dependent. Consequently, extraverted feelers tend to decide between right and wrong in each individual case, believing introverted feeling's insistence on universal judgments to be a bit dogmatic. For example, if an introverted feeler concludes that it is wrong to steal, she will apply that conclusion regardless of the circumstance. Fe, on the contrary, might be willing to make an exception for a homeless woman stealing a candy bar from a multi-billion-dollar corporation. If an introverted feeler is willing to make such an exception to her values, it will come as the result of extraverted perception offering new data for consideration, not because she changed her internal judgment for the object's sake. Fe, though, would have to rely on its introverted perception to give its judgments any of the sense of constancy naturally found in introverted feeling's approach.

While strong introverted feelers tend to be much more aware of their own feelings than extraverted feelers, Fe consistently displays greater awareness of other people's emotional states. Thus, Fe tends to be better at offering appropriate emotional support, guidance and sympathy — something that Fi struggles to do unless it has established a deep emotional rapport with the person who is suffering. However, Fe does not feel as deeply for others as introverted feeling does.

Introverted feelers will not share their empathy with those whom they believe have brought suffering on themselves unless the introverted feeler senses a deep personal connection; extraverted feelers will happily display sympathy in such a case, but they typically have no problem walking away and criticizing the sufferer quite ruthlessly for bringing trouble on himself.

While strong extraverted feelers tend to be quite adamant about upholding social norms and collective values, introverted feelers believe that such behavior restricts their freedom and autonomy far too much. It is not that strong extraverted feelers have no feelings or beliefs of their own; it is just that they are willing to overlook their personal feelings and beliefs for the sake of harmonious relationships. As a result, strong extraverted feelers play a central role in building and describing the morals, culture and values by which societies are defined.

Of all the functions, Fe is the least compatible with extraverted thinking because both functions aim to organize the outer world, but nonetheless focus on different aspects of reality. While extraverted thought focuses on impersonal systems, Fe works entirely in the world of people.

Extraverted judgment seeks closure, not because it believes there are no other options for consideration, but because it is necessary to make decisions to get things done in the world. Strong extraverted thinkers tend to see thought as belonging to everyone; the world behaves in measurable ways, regardless of people's individual thoughts. It does not matter if someone believes gravity is logically valid or dislikes the idea of falling because that person is still subject to gravity's laws. Conversely, strong extraverted feelers tend to hold that feelings and values belong to the group and they expect everyone to do what is needed to maintain a pleasant atmosphere.

As much as possible, Fe works to suppress its subjective aspect, introverted thinking, so that it can fulfill its mission: to make decisions in accord with communal values and needs.

Fe strives to match or alter the emotional vibe of a group. If someone is new to the group, the extraverted feeler will strive to make the new member feel welcome and help instill the group's values. Strong extraverted feelers typically feel comfortable establishing and enforcing a group's values, norms, and traditions. Enter the dark side of Fe. Strong extraverted feelers' skill at building positive group rapport also gives them the skill to do just the opposite, and the result is often the clique. Cliques are illustrative of Fe's constructive and destructive aspects. The very fact that a clique exists is testimony to shared ideas, values and experiences. The group's identity becomes so tightly defined that individual viewpoints within the group begin to merge into a collective whole. However, when a clique meets another, Fe's negative aspects sometimes come to the fore: losing track of opponents' individuality and unique value as human beings, emotional bullying and aggression, backbiting and manipulation, and all the worst kinds of groupthink. One often sees the same issues when communities, regions or countries are forced to interact. Culture wars are fought and permanently resolved via Fe. Strong extraverted feelers have no more of a dark side than any other type, but in light of so much discussion about Fe's skill at fostering harmony, it is necessary to point out its power of social manipulation.

Strong extraverted feelers do not cling to their values, in much the same way that extraverted thinkers do not cling to their thoughts. Strong extraverted judgment changes its views when the circumstances change. Accordingly, strong Fe-types not only preserve institutional values, but also can be trailblazers for social change when they recognize a pressing need in the world.

While Fe gives extraverted feelers a natural ease at understanding social dynamics and trends, it does little to ensure that its users have a sense of order in their inner worlds. Therefore, Fe needs a partner not only to assess logical validity, but also to provide the categories that underpin the outward expression of value judgments.

Anyone who uses Fe must also utilize introverted thinking since extraversion is opposed to introversion, as is feeling to thinking. Fe knows that the proper etiquette for a wedding is different than for a funeral because introverted thinking provides the categories and rules by which Fe expresses the appropriate feeling tones.

Fe can be quite demanding about following social rules and standards, and extraverted feelers will not hesitate to supply those who do not comply with the appropriate degree of social alienation. As a result, extraverted feelers can be quite demanding not only about upholding behavioral norms, but also about hygiene and cleanliness. Strong extraverted feelers' love of status symbols, like nice clothes, cars and houses, is only rivaled by that of strong extraverted sensors. To be fair, extraverted feelers are just as likely to choose a modest lifestyle so that they can focus on charity work. Underlying all of Fe's demands, though, is a subjective logical structure. The makings of good hygiene or the appropriate status symbols are derived by thinking judgments, which determine what is so or not so. The more extraverted feelers get in touch with their introverted thinking judgments, the more they will be able not only to apply value judgments consistently across broad contexts, but also to explain those judgments to others in a logically consistent way.

Fe is essential to the world, and everyone uses it to some degree. Without it, the glue that holds together families, communities, business organizations, cities and countries would not exist. Wherever there is sacrifice for the good of the group, demands for adherence to behavioral norms or sensitivity to cultural ebbs and flows, there too is Fe.

Introverted Thinking

Dominant: ISTP, INTP
Auxiliary: ESTP, ENTP
Tertiary: ISFJ, INFJ
Inferior: ESFJ, ENFJ

Introverted thinking, or Ti, is one of four introverted functions, and one of the four judging functions. Because Ti is concerned with the inner world, introverted thinkers prefer to deal with the universal aspects of logic.

Like extraverted thought, Ti focuses on definitions — defining true versus false, correct versus incorrect, here versus there. Unlike extraverted thought, Ti is not concerned with bringing order to the outer world, but to the inner. Hence, where extraverted thinking is highly concerned with facts, figures, rules and regulations, Ti sorts, categorizes and assesses the logical validity of propositions.

While extraverted thinking is highly attentive to empirical results, Ti is highly sensitive to logical consistency. This is because a fact derived from the outer world does not need logical support to be valid; a fact's very presence eliminates much of the need for formal logical analysis. On the other hand, Ti builds an internal framework piece by piece, utilizing ideas, analysis and logical deductions. Since Ti does not rely on empirical observations to determine the validity of an idea, introverted thinkers are quite careful to make sure only information that is fully vetted makes it into their models, thus ensuring that the models produce dependable results.

Similarly, introverted thinkers nitpick over word choice, spend pages defining a term for which extraverted thinkers believe a paragraph would suffice and construct theories that anticipate every special scenario or exception. While extraverted thinkers might believe that the hairsplitting is wasteful, introverted thinkers know that a failure to define terms sufficiently leads to nothing but confusion or failure. For example, where the extraverted thinker might be satisfied by the explanation that flipping a light switch causes the light to turn on or off, an introverted thinker wants to know the relationship between the switch and the light. Once Ti has worked that relationship out, the introverted thinker would want to know the connection between the switch and electricity, and so forth until Ti has a comprehensive understanding of the whole system. It should hardly be surprising, then, that strong introverted thinkers not only make the best philosophers, but also the best mechanics and repair people, especially when Ti is paired with solid sensing abilities.

Because Ti is oriented towards the subjective factor, most people tend to regard strong introverted thinkers as more open-minded and cosmopolitan in their views than are extraverted judgers. However, because extraverted judgment is attuned to the outside world, extraverted judgers are more than willing to alter their conclusions when new facts or data emerges; conclusions are merely tentative to the extraverted judger. Though Ti is slower to reach conclusions when compared to extraverted thinking or feeling, Ti will only alter its conclusions if a flaw in deductive logic is found. As a result, strong introverted thinkers are not nearly as open-minded as they might first seem.

Introverted thinkers tend to be passionate about learning, just like extraverted thinkers. However, introverted thinkers will often tackle a new topic simply for the sake of learning, while extraverted thinkers tend to learn a new subject out of a belief that it will help them accomplish their goals. It is not that introverted thinkers have no goals; instead, introverted thinkers are primarily interested in using logic to enhance their self-knowledge, not to advance an agenda in the outer world.

Of all the functions, Ti is the least compatible with introverted feeling since both functions work to order the inner world but are nonetheless organizing different content. Because introverted feeling and Ti judge inwardly, there is not much in the way of outward conflict to observe between them. However,

Ti has little use for what it would deem as introverted feeling's overly personalized approach to values.

That is because introverted feelers strive to structure their inner worlds according to what feels right to them, but introverted thinking uses logic to structure the inner world in a rather cold way. Introverted thinkers, therefore, do not take expert opinion, professional guidance or so-called scientific proof as gospel. Ti insists that all incoming information must be worked through its model, and only the information that survives this process will be accepted as valid.

As much as possible, Ti works to suppress its objective aspect, extraverted feeling, so that it can fulfill its purpose: to make decisions that are in tune with the rules of logical validity.

Ti wants to find the very essence of ideas, much as introverted intuition does. Where introverted intuition enters the idea, looks around and rearranges the furniture just to see what happens, Ti wants to break the idea down into logical truths that can be applied in a variety of contexts. Ti's process does not give introverted thinkers flashes of insight that reveal the idea's core, rather every bit of understanding is the hard-won result of conscious analysis. Consequently, introverted thinkers are typically quite good at explaining how they reached their conclusions; but introverted thinkers do not seek to impose their conclusions on others, no matter how strong their conclusions might be. Introverted thinkers seek only to understand fully all the implications of their ideas. That is not to suggest that introverted thinkers have no respect for facts; it is just that facts merely provide the substance for introverted thinkers' deliberations. Ti knows that lacking a clear understanding of a fact's causal mechanisms and context, it can never derive universally applicable insights. For Ti, a logically valid argument is proof enough, and introverted thinkers are just as brutal in their conclusions as are extraverted thinkers; introverted thinkers simply do not feel the need to express their conclusions to those with whom they do not share a rapport.

Strong introverted thinking is incredibly methodical, and introverted thinkers expect others to respect Ti's individual approach and ideas. Fundamental to formal logical analysis is the ability to break things down into categories. Though certain categories might have some objective validity, the categories' only reality is psychic, i.e., categories do not exist in the outer world, objects do. Nevertheless, categories have a reality substantial enough that a choice to categorize something one way or another can result in sweeping changes to any conclusions. What that means in practice is that Ti, though aware of the object, always begins and ends its work with subjectively held principles.

While Ti provides introverted thinkers with a deep and detailed understanding of their ideas, beliefs, assumptions and theories, Ti is unable to resolve all of life's problems by itself. Ti needs a partner that is skilled at not only assessing values and emotions, but also structuring the outer world.

Every person who uses introverted thinking must also use extraverted feeling since introversion is opposed to extraversion, as is thinking to feeling.

A crucial aspect of the human experience is the ability to relate to others. Key to relating to others is the ability to understand other people's values, emotions and motivations. Ti, however, is in no way qualified to forge such relationships. Moreover, if Ti lacked the outlet through which it could express its judgments to the world, the world would not stand to benefit from Ti's unsurpassed insight into the singular value of logical validity.

Ti can be incredibly picky about following formal grammatical conventions and strictly utilizing dictionary definitions. The introverted thinker who has taken the time to analyze such preferences has surely realized that while the rules of grammar certainly constitute a logical system, grammar is not logical per se. That is, the laws that undergird proper grammatical expression could have easily been designed in a completely different fashion. Thus, grammar is merely a logical expression of society's high valuation of clear communication. Similarly, trees are not called trees because it is logical to do so; everyone agrees to the word tree because by doing so, communication is facilitated. Dependence on these kinds of social norms is central to Ti's work, and strong Ti-types tend to manifest extraverted feeling as a deep, but often unconscious, respect for the values and beliefs that bind society together.

There is an infinite amount of material for Ti to ponder. Since Ti does not have the time to find the essence of every idea, extraverted feeling steps in to help introverted thinkers decide which ideas they would enjoy solving most. It turns out that the problems that strong introverted thinkers find most interesting are the issues that are troubling their families, organizations and communities.

Since all people use Ti to some extent, the world would not be the same without it. This function is used whenever one assesses logical validity, attempts to explain the causes behind a phenomenon or breaks an idea down into its constituent elements.

Myers and Briggs's JP Axis

By this point, the core of psychological type theory has been outlined in-depth. It might be surprising, then, that in her book, *Gifts Differing*, Myers argued that her judging-perceiving, or JP axis "completes the structure of type. . . . This preference is indispensable for ascertaining which process is dominant,"[21] even asserting that Jung's *Psychological Types* "never discusses the introvert's extraversion."

It is incorrect to assert that the "JP preference completes the structure of type" because this axis was never separate from any type's structure to begin with; each person thinks and feels, so each person judges; and everyone uses both sensing and intuition, so everyone perceives. Moreover, Jung dedicates a whole subchapter of *Psychological Types* to the "introvert's extraversion."[22]

More so than any other factor, Myers and Briggs's addition of this dichotomy has both served to popularize Jung's theory and confuse those who are learning about typology. Myers wrote that judging types "are more decisive than curious" and perceptive types "are more curious than decisive." Judging types "live according to plans, standards, and customs not easily or lightly set aside, to which the situation of the moment must, if possible, be made to conform." Perceptive types "live according to the situation of the moment and adjust themselves easily to the accidental and the unexpected."[23]

Because *Gifts Differing's* definitions of judging and perceiving are quite simple, everyone should find some truth in them. The problem is, the definitions are simple to the point of being incomplete. The perceiving-judging dichotomy, when properly understood, provides a powerful tool for ascertaining one's type. However, most people do not dig deeply enough into the theory to understand fully the nuances involved. Moreover, some of the logical assumptions at work behind Myers and Briggs's addition of this dichotomy are questionable.

Gifts Differing's conception of the perceiving-judging axis merely describes the function a type is best at extraverting, i.e., the face each type shows the world. Thus, Myers's description of this axis is not oriented to one's true psychology, but to appearances. In extraverted types, the strongest extraverted function is the dominant function. Introverted types' best extraverted function is, obviously enough, not the dominant function, but the auxiliary.

All introverted types have a four-letter combination of either IxxJ or IxxP. While IJ-types extravert their judgment, their dominant process is always introverted perception. On the other hand, IP-types extravert a perceptive process, but their dominant process is always introverted judgment. This means that IJ-types are far more open-minded than their EJ brethren because EJ-types' dominant process is extraverted judgment. For example, ESTJ and ISTJ both use the same cognitive functions, but ESTJ's dominant process is extraverted thinking, while ISTJ's is introverted sensing; and ESTJ's auxiliary process is introverted sensing, while ISTJ's auxiliary is extraverted thought.

Similarly, IP-types are not nearly as open-minded as EP-types. For example, ESFP and ISFP share the same cognitive functions, but ESFP's dominant process is extraverted sensing, while ISFP's is introverted feeling; and ESFP use auxiliary introverted feeling, while ISFP use extraverted sensing in the auxiliary position. Thus, one could make the argument that IJ-types are similarly open-minded as EP-types, but when dealing with the outer world, IJ-types prefer closure; and IP-types seek closure just as much as EJ-types, but when dealing with the outer world, IP-types like to keep their options open.

The auxiliary process is always subject to the dominant function's decrees. As a result, IJ-types might use judgment to structure the outer world, but it is inaccurate to refer to them as judging types. IP-types might like to keep their options open in the outer world, but because the IP dominant process is always judgment, it is more accurate to think of them as judging types. Consequently, popular understanding of this axis is accurate only for the extraverted types, while it perpetuates half-truths about the introverted types.

To be fair, Myers wrote that her JP axis only refers to appearances, so if someone digs far enough if into her work, this distinction is perfectly clear. However, if Myers knew that her conception of the JP axis only describes appearances, why would she still choose to apply this axis in the manner she did? The best guess is that by highlighting appearances, it might be easier to type oneself or others. The tradeoff, of course, is a diminished capacity for using the theory as a tool for increasing self-knowledge.

In addition to Myers and Briggs's interpretation of Jung's theory, there is another model referred to as socionics. Socionics's interpretation of Jung's work also results in a JP axis, but instead of applying only to appearances, socionics's JP axis describes whether the dominant function is a judging process or a perceiving process. One can tell whether one is dealing with socionics's interpretation of Jung's work or Myers and Briggs's from the capitalization of each type's code. For example, Myers and Briggs's ESTJ would be ESTj in socionics, ESFP would become ESFp. The letters stay the same because ESTJ is a dominant judging type and ESFP is a dominant perceiving type.

The real magic happens with the introverted types. Myers and Briggs's IJ-types become Ixxp, while the IP-types become Ixxj. The lowercase "p" serves to highlight IJ-types' dominant perception, while lowercase "j" is indicative of IP-types' dominant judgment. Thus, INTJ are INTp in socionics since both use dominant introverted intuition. INFP would be INFj in socionics since this type uses dominant introverted feeling.

The Shadow, Socionics and Beebe

Though each person has some degree of conscious access to four cognitive functions, it is necessary that all eight cognitive functions operate within the psyche. In socionics, the cognitive functions are referred to as *information elements*. Because socionics originated abroad, there are some minor differences in the descriptions of the information elements as opposed to the cognitive functions found in most other resources on Jungian types. In the essential components, however, the information elements are at one with a competent description of the cognitive functions. If that were not so, socionics would have no relation to Jung's theory because it is from the cognitive functions, and their interactions, that the theory of types necessarily follows.

When one internalizes the nature of the cognitive functions, it becomes clear that each function provides information of the highest importance to one's understanding of the world. Thus, socionics holds that the information elements make up the eight aspects of reality. Jung surely agreed with this because he wrote, "the objective stimulus is absolutely necessary to [introverted] sensation and merely produces something different from what the external situation might lead one to expect."[24] For these reasons, it is a shame that Myers did not spend more time describing the role every function plays in each type's mind, only dedicating one page of *Gifts Differing* to what she called the shadow—a page that altogether fails to discuss what she means by the term shadow.

It is true that the four functions that lie in the unconscious have shadowy elements; that should hardly be surprising since one can clearly see the outlines of the shadow in the inferior function. Assimilating the inferior function into the psyche is the prerequisite for seeing these four hidden functions at work within oneself. That is not to say that one needs to master the inferior, one simply needs to observe, accept and willingly utilize the inferior's point of view at the right times.

Because the four functions concealed beneath the inferior are profoundly unconscious, their use is typically undifferentiated and clumsy. It would be well to remember, then, that each function is essentially the same in both its introverted and extraverted standpoints; it is merely the direction in which libido flows that distinguishes them. For example, introverted feeling and extraverted feeling are essentially the same process because both functions aim to establish values—extraverted feeling striving to structure the outer world and introverted feeling, the inner world. That means that by reaching a level of self-awareness that allows one to get a sense of these hidden functions' workings, the four conscious functions are further developed. For example, extraverted thinkers will be more effective decision makers if they have strong deductive logic in addition to empirical validation. Similarly, introverted thinkers' deductive analysis is strengthened, not hindered, by recognizing when their conclusions mesh with the observable facts. There are many benefits to reaching such a degree of psychic organization.

Socionics's most important contribution to psychological typing is that socionics provides a way by which Jung's type theory can be united with Freud's model of the psyche. The following chart not only represents the traditional approach to structuring the cognitive functions, but also represents the extent to which most can develop consciously:

DOMINANT	AUXILIARY
TERTIARY	INFERIOR

Socionics uses what it calls the Model A to organize the information elements differently, and results in slightly differing concepts of each information element's role in the psyche.

EGO	LEADING	CREATIVE
SUPER EGO	VULNERABLE	ROLE
SUPER ID	MOBILIZING	SUGGESTIVE
ID	IGNORING	DEMONSTRATIVE

Since socionics uses terms that might be unfamiliar to many students of type theory, consider the Model A using Myers and Briggs's terminology. In this model, the word *anti* should be taken to mean the function in its opposing attitude. Hence, a type whose dominant function is Se would have an anti-dominant of Si, while a type with inferior Fi would have anti-inferior Fe.

EGO	DOMINANT	AUXILIARY
SUPER EGO	ANTI-TERTIARY	ANTI-INFERIOR
SUPER ID	TERTIARY	INFERIOR
ID	ANTI-DOMINANT	ANTI-AUXILIARY

According to Freud, the psyche is divisible into three parts: superego, ego and id.[25] To Freud, every child's psychological development begins with the id, which represents the archaic, instinctual part of the human psyche that is concerned only with perpetuating survival by means of the pleasure/pain principle. The id does not care about how realistic its desires might be or other people's needs; it simply seeks immediate gratification and operates according to the famous pleasure principle.[26]

Freud believed that the superego, on the contrary, constitutes one's conscience and, as such a moral compass, it helps to moderate the id's instinctive brutality by considering the impact not only on oneself, but on society. The ego serves as the bridge between the id's desires and the superego's insistence on moral perfection. Like the id, the ego strives to maximize pleasure and minimize pain; the ego, however, strives to meet the id's desires in moral ways. Thus, if the id sees a gold watch that it likes, it would be fine with taking the watch by force. The ego, however, would derive socially acceptable ways to get the watch, like saving money, taking out a loan or selling property to get the cash. The ego does not make such efforts because the ego cares about right and wrong in and of itself, but because of the influence of the superego combined with the ego's real-world experience.

From Freud, one already gets a strong sense of socionics's use of the above terms. Socionics holds that the ego block consists of two functions: the leading function and creative function. The ego block is always a person's preferred way of seeing and dealing with the world at large. Stereotypes surrounding each psychological type are largely based on this block of functions. Moreover, people tend to talk about their ego block when asked to describe themselves. Since this block only supplies direct information about 25 percent of reality, or two of eight information elements, exclusive reliance on the ego block will result both in specific skills developed because of extensive practice, but also special liabilities caused by inadequate conscious recognition of all aspects of reality.

Socionics's utilization of the term superego is especially apt. The superego block is made up of information elements utterly opposed to the ego block and, thus, socionics states that one's use of the superego block will be limited. For example, ESTP's ego block holds Se and Ti, but their superego block consists of Ne and Fi. Recall from the foregoing discussion about the cognitive functions, no function is more at odds with Se than Ne, and no function is as opposed to Fi as Ti. As a result, ESTP tend to feel that Ne and Fi are, at once, things to be loathed and ideals to which ESTP strive. The super id block is unique to socionics. While it is quite difficult to use the superego block to operate consciously in the world, socionics states that people are more conscious of the superego block than they are of their super id, which is composed of the tertiary and inferior functions. The reason is not that people are generally more skilled in use of the superego than the super id. On the contrary, most people's *use* of the superego can best be described as disastrous and incompetent. Instead, people tend to become incredibly aware of their inadequate skill with the superego block and, thus, spend their time avoiding situations that demand it, or doing their best to strengthen their ability to meet the superego's inherently moral demands competently. Almost no matter how strong the effort, most people revert to the ego's favored territory. This makes sense if one remembers from earlier that the super id (i.e., the tertiary and inferior functions) tends to be felt as childlike because its functions are undifferentiated.

The superego block consists of the role and vulnerable functions, or anti-inferior and anti-tertiary functions. The vulnerable function, in particular, is a sore spot for every type. Many refer to this function as the point of least resistance because direct criticism about its use is quite painful. Thus, people tend to comply resentfully with the vulnerable function's demands or refuse to meet its demands altogether. People also show a degree of unease with their role function because its use is anathema to their preferred way of metabolizing information, which is through the dominant function. When criticized for their role function's shortcomings, mature adults are bothered little because they are already aware of the shortcoming and have likely found ways to make up for the weakness by relying on a combination of their super id and ego blocks.

Last, the id block consists of the ignoring and demonstrative functions, or the anti-dominant and anti-auxiliary. Though the use of these functions tends to be profoundly unconscious, people nevertheless show real skill using these functions in short bursts. However, people often consider their ignoring and demonstrative functions' input irrelevant because these functions operate in the opposite attitude of the ego block. In practice, that means it takes a great deal of libido to access these functions for any length of time. Thus, most people have no idea the breadth of skills to which these functions could give access.

Considering the above, socionics is clearly a superior functional interpretation of Jung's theory to Myers and Briggs's because socionics attempts to account for the way people metabolize information about all eight aspects of reality, not simply four. In fact, socionics has gone far beyond the scope of Jung's theory since socionics has additional dichotomies and addresses intertype relations, which it uses to discuss the archetypal patterns that emerge when one type interacts with another.

Socionics is not the only interpretation of Jung's work that aims to account for each cognitive function's role in consciousness. John Beebe, an expert on Jungian psychology, also has a wonderful eight-function model. Though Beebe's interpretation is not as readily reconciled with Freud's framework of the psyche as socionics, Beebe's model has the advantage of simplicity and, unlike socionics, does not get overly determinative about the nature of the types and their relationships, relationships that are always influenced by everyone's unique experiences. Instead, Beebe relies on the most axiomatic principles of Jung's type theory as well as Jung's work on the nature of the unconscious.

Beebe rightly argues that each cognitive function is carried by an archetypal complex, thus making each function something of a mini personality.

We also, by definition, have to have 8 complexes carrying those types, or blocks, or associated with those types or blocks. We have – all of us – 8 basic intelligences that make up the totality of our potential for conscious functioning.

The system of psychological types is simply an archetypal model that organizes those 8 basic units into some kind of structure. Now, there are a lot of arguments about what that basic structure is, but there is no argument that there are these 8 basic intelligences.[27]

While it is, therefore, correct to acknowledge that each cognitive function has a nature that, at least from a theoretical perspective, is unique and definable, every type's relationship to each function depends on the complex that carries it in consciousness. For example, INTJ have quite a different relationship to Ni than ESFP. Through profound self-reflection and clinical observations, Beebe came to define the archetypal complexes that carry the cognitive functions.

Beebe states that the dominant function carries the hero/heroine archetype.[28] One feels deeply at ease, in command and up to any challenge when using the dominant function. When one feels the need to rescue oneself or those whom one values, this function steps in to save the day. The auxiliary function corresponds with the good father/mother archetype. It is used to provide advice and guidance to oneself and others in a positive, growth-based direction.

Beebe refers to the tertiary function as the puer/puella or child archetype, an acknowledgement of a child's tremendous creative power when given proper parenting, and the child's near-singular ability to trip over his own feet when the parent is away.

Last among the four conscious functions is the inferior function, which Beebe refers to as the anima/animus archetype. The anima and animus are of incredible significance in Jung's work, as these two archetypes form the bridge from the shadow, or personal unconscious, through the collective unconscious[29] and to the psychological fact Jung called "self." Jung held that every man has an inner feminine nature and each woman has an inner masculine nature. The anima compels men to seek out a relatedness (feminine principle or blurring of the edges) to the world around them, while the animus drives women to discrimination and analysis (masculine principle or sharpening of the edges). The stereotypical male's outward aggression is balanced by an inner feminine nature, which explains why men sometimes clam up when their egos are attacked and often begin pouting in a way that is supposedly characteristic of a woman. On the other hand, the stereotypical view of women as gentle and nurturing is balanced by an inner masculine nature, which explains why women often become confrontational when their egos are attacked or endangered.

Again, everyone has a limited degree of conscious access to the inferior function. Hence, the inferior function does not constitute the shadow, as some might have people think. The inferior does, however, clearly border the shadow, and might even slightly overlap it in some cases. The remaining four functions are, more or less, fully in the shadow for every person. Those who have gained some conscious access to these shadow functions' workings are not conscious of them in a strict sense. These functions' archetypal materials tend to come to the surface in dreams, fantasy and works of art. To be conscious of one's shadow is rather like being aware that the sun is still shining at night; one really cannot see the sun when it is dark outside, though one might know that the sun is still shining as brilliantly as ever. Similarly, one might come to recognize one's shadow quite well through brutal self-analysis and a real commitment to understanding all the fantasy material the unconscious might produce, but no matter how much of the unconscious material is consciously understood, there is always more unconscious material to be found. Most often, these shadowy functions are projected onto others to avoid much of the pain of looking within—forgetting that there is much joy within, too. In such cases, one might conclude that another's argument is stupid when, in fact, it could be one's own lack of understanding that is truly to blame. Such projections, while great at preventing wounds to the ego, are injurious to the full flowering of the conscious mind and explain why many never perceive their golden flower.[30]

The first of the shadow functions Beebe calls the opposing personality archetype because it opposes the dominant function. This function consists of material repressed by the dominant function—repressed because the dominant function is taking the libido necessary to bring this opposing personality to consciousness. Thus, one tends to project this anti-dominant function onto others quite readily. The second archetype is that of the senex or witch, otherwise known as the anti-auxiliary function; and as is to be expected, this archetypal complex is used to criticize or dogmatically find fault with oneself and others; the senex/witch is especially used to reject information that one does not want to hear. Third is the anti-tertiary, or trickster archetype, which is certainly a nod to how frustrating this archetype can be when one is forced to use it or when another is observed using it in a seemingly over-the-top way. Nevertheless, the trickster archetypal complex often helps one exploit norms associated with a cognitive function's use. INTJ, for example, might exploit, even unconsciously, people's expectations about decency in the workplace to leverage a promotion or opportunity that would have been unavailable if the INTJ played strictly by the rules. Last in this chthonic region is the daemon archetype, or anti-inferior function, which is always the function most strongly opposed to the dominant function's preferred mode of operation, and thus, quite prone to projection. This daemon archetype has a way of not only making one look like the class dunce, but also providing the most unexpected solutions to life's problems—when one is quiet enough to hear this archetype's voice.

It is important to note that Beebe is not overly committed about the order in which these shadow functions fall in the psyche; the order given is simply there to help assimilate the information. However, if Jung's theories regarding the compensatory relationship between the conscious and unconscious minds are a guidepost, one can expect the shadow function's order to be in direct opposition to the conscious preferences.

Because Beebe's model accounts for every cognitive function's operation, it is also superior to Myers and Briggs's four-function model. Whether one prefers socionics or Beebe is a matter of personal preference, and both models provide much that is deserving of investigation. It is worth noting, however, that Beebe's model is more useful as a tool for self-exploration since Beebe explains the archetypal forces at work within each individual in a concise fashion. On the other hand, socionics is more useful for the exploration of relationship dynamics because socionics has systematized the archetypes at work between each type and all the others. For those reasons, one might also posit that Beebe would be a good launching point for extraverts who are looking to increase the scope of their conscious minds since Beebe looks at the inner world; socionics, then, would be a good place to start for introverts who are looking to grow since intertype relationships necessarily take place within objective reality's domain.

Psychology of Si-Ne, Fe-Ti Types

ISFJ

SI	FE
TI	NE
SE	FI
TE	NI

ISFJ are primarily oriented toward their inner worlds through Si and, to a lesser degree, Ti. Fi and Ni operate unconsciously.

With Si as the dominant function, every other function is necessarily subordinate to its demands.

In the simplest terms, Si maps one's sensory experience and focuses its direct attention not on tangible reality, but the effect tangible reality has on the subject. In more philosophical terms, Si is the vehicle that allows one to experience the universals of sensory experience—a statement that seems to be contradictory. When people experience the outside world, however, they never encounter things like cold or hot, high or low, as these are mere abstractions; and determining whether things are hot or cold, high or low, is completely a matter of one's perspective. To one person, it is hot outside if it is 85 degrees yet, to another, that sounds like a comfortable day. Despite the abstract nature of things like hotness and coldness, all people would agree that an ice cube is cold insofar as it participates in coldness and a burning coal is hot insofar as it participates in hotness—relative to human skin, of course. Si tunes into this unique side of sensory experience, experience in which it is not the ice cube or burning coal that is of interest, but the universals that those particular objects allow people to experience—and those experiences are at least as much psychological as physiological. It is for these reasons that Jung wrote of Si's view of the world being akin to the way a million-year-old person would sense the world.[31] With Si in ISFJ's driver seat, members of this type are deeply in tune with their experience of the world and, therefore, seek physical comfort, stability and safety. Their comfort-seeking tendencies generally manifest as a passion for tradition. Si seeks to maintain customs because, with the outer world being such an unstable and unpredictable place, customs lend a sense of constancy and regularity; holidays, birthdays and graduations, thus, take on special significance, as do rules, authority and institutions. Avoiding risks wherever possible, Si compels ISFJ to take the tried-and-true approach—taking out life insurance, establishing rainy-day funds, saving for college.

ISFJ are deeply in tune with their inner sensory experience, but that experience would be unassimilable without a function to structure it.

Not only is Ti ISFJ's tertiary function, it is also this type's chief introverted judging function. ISFJ's efforts at finding internal order thus center around clarifying terms, categorizing conceptual links and uncovering root assumptions. Though the tertiary function rarely shows real signs of differentiation, it is still a workhorse in the psychic landscape. As is typical with either of the introverted judging functions, ISFJ can be quite dogged and inflexible in their internal judgments—a problem that is in no way mitigated by Si's penchant for conservation. Introverted functions, especially judging functions, are prone to an imperviousness to the outside world, often setting subjective considerations so far above concrete evidence that many judgments are not subject to modification in the least. While ISFJ are far less prone to that issue than types whose introverted judgment occupies the inferior role (EJ types), a degree of stubbornness is still noted, even when in error. ISFJ are most at home with Ti when they use it to ascertain the rules and structure that allow for effective communication and smooth interactions.

Because Fi operates in their psychological shadow, ISFJ tend to be much more emotionally nurturing and supportive of others than they are of themselves. This is because, to ISFJ, feelings and values belong to the group and ISFJ can hardly think of anything more distasteful, disconcerting or even dreadful than holding feelings or values that seem to push ISFJ away from their families, organizations or communities. Fi, however, is driven by authenticity, by integrity to one's own truth, motivations and ideals. ISFJ tend to reserve Fi's use for criticism, both of themselves and others. Others are privy to this display only when ISFJ have been pushed to the limits. The fastest way to bring this dark side out of ISFJ is to assault their logical frameworks (Ti), whether directly or indirectly—the indirect form occurring by subjecting ISFJ to a failure to adhere to foundational collective norms, which are necessarily undergirded by a subjective reasoning. At such times, people can get a clear sense of where they really stand with ISFJ since their normally elegant social mask is ripped off in favor of displays of righteous indignation and occasional vitriol. Ni, on the other hand, is far more challenging for members of this type, who in most cases find Ni's speculative habits not only irrelevant, but also insufficiently grounded in history and practical experience. Ni treats the past as a mere launching point, looking at experience as important, but overrated. To ISFJ, therefore, Ni is bizarre. This problem is made worse by the fact that no function is as strongly opposed to this type's dominant function as Ni.

ISFJ's outer psychology consists of Fe and Ne, while Se and Te operate unconsciously. With Fe as the lead extraverted function, ISFJ are focused on people, considering not only how ISFJ may serve others, but also how ISFJ, themselves, stand to benefit by the harmonious management of human interactions and relationships. To strong Te-types, who often manage the outside world by mitigating the human element, such a people-based approach to handling life must surely seem strange and inefficient. ISFJ, however, are not driven by efficiency. Instead, they are driven by a need to uphold the values that were instilled in them from their childhoods, values ISFJ not only expect themselves to live up to, but others as well. Deeply in tune with the appropriate social protocols, ISFJ not only derive their values objectively, i.e., from their friends, families, communities and jobs, ISFJ also play an essential role in ensuring the community's values are passed down to the next generation in one form or another. Fe is no less aggressive in its efforts to structure the outer world than Te, but instead of giving direct orders as is common of strong Te, Fe-types are quite good at couching an order in language that makes the directive seem like a suggestion. "John, I don't know that a bottle of wine is a good gift for a baby shower," an ISFJ might say. "Don't you think we should get some toys for the baby instead?"

ISFJ's leadership style—their way of organizing the outer world—shows a good deal of Ne's influence, which treats the world not as a place of certainty, but as a simmering cauldron of possibilities. Since Ne is ISFJ's inferior function, it typically shows little evidence of differentiation and, therefore, most of the possibilities ISFJ envision are of the negative variety. Ne operates objectively, with an eye towards the ceaseless process of becoming, working with ideas and abstractions in a way analogous to the way Se-types address tangible reality. Though ISFJ rarely show the degree of intellectual elasticity demonstrated among strong Ne-types, ISFJ's ideas are far more grounded in practical experience and, because of the strength of their extraverted judgment, ISFJ tend to be better at concretizing their ideas, making a much higher percentage of their ideas real than would be seen in strong Ne-types, for whom an idea or possibility is interesting only as long as it is a potentiality, not a reality. Because of Ne, ISFJ often get a vague but powerful sense of what to expect next. However, ISFJ's skills at prediction are most accurate when they have a good degree of familiarity with the emergent possibilities.

Because it is so closely related to their dominant function, ISFJ often show some competence with Se, even though the function is firmly entrenched in ISFJ's unconscious. Though ISFJ are acutely aware of the effect the world has on their physical organism, they often have much less awareness of tangible reality. To ISFJ, it must seem a bit strange that many people are highly attuned to the outer world yet have little conscious awareness of how the world affects them. This dynamic means ISFJ have little interest in seeking out the latest thrills and frills, and this type prizes tradition, routine, history and the comfort that accompanies such values. While strong Se-types are unperturbed by novelty, risks or sensory extremes, ISFJ's constant attention to maintaining their physical equilibrium means they view anything unfamiliar or strange with deep suspicion. Te, however, is ISFJ's most frustrating cognitive function. Te structures the outside world impersonally, looking at systems and laws that are meant not only to standardize vast swaths of the human experience, but also ensure accountability for any behavior that undermines the system. ISFJ look at laws and policies as expressions of collective values. Child labor is not illegal because it is illogical, for example; in fact, logic has nothing to say on this matter. Child labor is illegal because society values the education, nurturing and development of its children far more than the immediate, but short-sighted, benefits that come from exploiting those who are most vulnerable. Because ISFJ favor Fe over Te, they tend to view strong Te-types as putting the law above the values it is meant to protect. ISFJ, thus, tend to focus on sharing the importance of the values that hold groups, businesses and communities together, and enforce the rules not with the possibility of codified punishments or imprisonment, but with the appropriate degree of social isolation, which for strong Fe-types is unbearable and, for strong Te-types, little more than an inconvenience.

When ISFJ's inner and outer psychologies are combined, one finds natural guardians—guardians of society, its institutions and the human spirit. ISFJ are in tune with the way the world has always been, for ISFJ's experience of the world does not reside outside of them but forms a core part of their identity. For ISFJ, therefore, protecting society's institutions and fighting for fundamental collective values are synonymous with fighting for themselves. ISFJ's protective efforts are always performed in service of the group, as ISFJ are passionate about protecting the values and traditions that tie people together, and ISFJ quickly adjust their own behavior to meet established norms and standards. Mature ISFJ are methodical, and because they realize the necessity of effective communication to maintaining healthy relationships and strong communities, ISFJ spend a lot of time clarifying terms, building logical frameworks and determining the most effective way to apply their values to the world. Despite their warm and friendly approach, ISFJ do not appreciate being told how or what to think; they reach their conclusions themselves and they let others do the same — as long as everyone follows the appropriate social protocols and customs. ISFJ tend to believe the greatest threat to the institutions, places and people who ISFJ value comes from risk, most often risks from poorly considered change, and it is risk and unpredictable change that ISFJ seek to eliminate.

ISFJ's perceptions are highly polarized toward their dominant Si and, therefore, away from their inferior Ne. This kind of polarization is nothing to be ashamed of; it is merely the hallmark of this type. ISFJ are highly attached to the symbols that make up their lives: families, homes, credentials and histories. Unlike ENTP, who use all the same functions, but in the reverse order, ISFJ do not see these symbols as a launching pad for exploration, but as the very core of ISFJ's everyday experience. From their cherished symbols, ISFJ derive a sense of stability and rootedness. This type is most comfortable using intuition in forming associations to symbols. ISFJ see a picture, and it brings back a flood of memories from that day, from the sun shining down on them at the beach, to the topics of conversation, to what they had for dinner. ISFJ are less comfortable using their intuitions to determine what will happen, and they have a habit of envisioning that the future will be like the past. To the extent they seriously deal with the future, ISFJ see nothing but risks and opportunities for disaster, which distinguishes them from Ne-dominant types, who instead, see opportunities as things to be exploited, not feared. While ISFJ can be warm and friendly, they sometimes struggle with surprise and spontaneity; they are most comfortable not only when they know what to expect, but also when topics of conversation center around familiar and uncontentious themes.

ISFJ show far less polarization in their judgment dichotomy because their dominant function prevents auxiliary Fe from robbing the libido tertiary Ti needs to reach consciousness. ISFJ are well in tune with their groups' values, feelings and motivations, but they are not as deeply involved in the social scene as their ESFJ counterparts. ISFJ are very comfortable giving direction, but much prefer that everyone simply does what is right. Esteeming their time for reflection, mature ISFJ can be very analytical, working hard to use the right words at the right times, and ensuring conceptual frameworks have a basic level of logical consistency. ISFJ are most comfortable applying their logic to their relationships and beliefs — deciding what values to appeal to, reflecting on what a mission statement says about an institution's values and commitment to the community. While ISFJ can be insistent on everyone working to maintain a harmonious and peaceful environment, ISFJ are generally much more comfortable letting people display their true feelings than ESFJ, both because ISFJ are not as strong as ESFJ in their extraverted judgments, and because ISFJ are better in tune with their own introverted judgments.

INTP

TI	NE
SI	FE
TE	NI
SE	FI

INTP are chiefly oriented toward their inner worlds through Ti and, to a lesser extent, their tertiary function, Si. Ni and Fi are used unconsciously.

With Ti as the dominant function, every other function is necessarily subordinate to its demands.

Ti internally deduces the structure, laws and logic that underlie experience, whether the experience be internal or external. With its natural tendency to find even the smallest distinctions, no other function rivals Ti's capacity to select the precise word to communicate its intent or easily find the right answer by discarding data that is irrelevant to its exploration. To INTP, however, data cannot be irrelevant in an absolute sense, just relatively so; and, consequently, INTP will often continue processing such data, asking what-if questions and working to discover the contexts in which the data would prove useful. In this regard, INTP differ significantly from their shadow type, ENTJ, whose logical exploration is limited to what will achieve the desired result—ending all consideration of a matter when it becomes apparent that it will not yield the right outcome. With its closed system of logic, Ti can come across as all too willing to discard real-world facts in service of supporting a theoretical insight or conclusion, but this is a difficulty that mature INTP have overcome—a result of INTP's deep and fundamental value of truth, a value that INTP acquire from the community. Because logic is internally held for Ti-types, INTP who have strong mathematical backgrounds could easily imagine a world that follows a whole new set of physics, explaining its rules with perfect logical coherence down to the smallest details—an exercise that must seem absurd to most Te users.

With this incredible ability to deduce laws that are logical, but that might nonetheless ill accord with the outer world, INTP need some way to ensure that their train of thought does not go off the rails—a way to ensure that their thoughts follow a traditional and orderly model. When it comes to their frameworks, INTP can be quite stubborn, for while the mature ones readily acknowledge that there are as many paths to truth as there are truth seekers, INTP still tend to believe that they have chosen the most logical path, especially if that path has consistently led to the correct conclusions in the past.

This is because Si, with its acute awareness of the internal sensory experience, seeks and cherishes comfort, tending to believe that traditions should be followed simply because they have led to reliable results before. Si minimizes risk and follows the tried-and-true path. INTP are, therefore, not only deeply wed to the people, places and things they have enjoyed, but also to the systems of logical exploration, categorization, hypothesizing and synthesizing that have traditionally proved effective. INTP, then, are deeply conservative people, regardless of their politics—working to conserve fundamental logical conclusions, perspectives and, at times, core collective values. This drive to conservation is not applied to the outer world, but

INTP's inner world, which is profoundly ordered and organized, regardless of INTP's outer appearance. If one could imagine ENTJ's fierce drive to structure the outer world, one can get a sense of how this internal process of deriving and keeping order plays out in INTP's psychology. For example, while INTP rarely reject someone's offer of information outright, INTP's judgment of the information's usefulness to themselves is just as brutal and unfeeling as is outwardly observed in ENTJ.

Ni allows INTP to define experience using and according to symbols that are deeply personal. A symbol does not have to be a mere drawing on a piece of paper. All sensory experience is symbolic; the meaning derived from those symbols is psychic, whether the meaning is expressed objectively, in terms of possibilities, or subjectively, in terms of underlying cohesiveness. The latter is Ni's nature. INTP's primary use of Ni is to criticize themselves or others. At such times, INTP can draw a morbid picture that accounts for every aspect of one's failure; and worse, they can build that picture from the tiniest scrap of data, made into a symbol that unifies the experience. INTP, on the other hand, are far less skilled with their own feelings, values and morals (Fi). When it comes to ethics, INTP are more comfortable deriving them from the outer world — this type's explanations of right and wrong often limited to the most cursory offering of a cliché that sums up the value in question. That there might be a system of ethics that, though it might be personal and unique to themselves, might transcend the collective's understanding of right and wrong is of little concern or importance to INTP—an oddity given that it is just INTP's willingness to believe that their own systems of thought surpass the collective's that has led so many INTP, like Einstein, to alter radically the collective's point of view.

INTP's outer psychology consists of Ne and Fe, while Te and Se operate unconsciously. With Ne as the lead extraverted function, INTP are focused on possibilities, potentialities and opportunities. Abstractions and ideas fascinate them. INTP's inner desire for stability and tradition are belied by Ne's opposing desire for exploration and originality. As the only other type that uses Ti in the dominant position, ISTP are equally concerned with logic, but because ISTP use auxiliary Se instead of Ne, their logic is applied to matters that are concrete and empirical, not abstract. Despite INTP's strong psychological organization, they do not typically structure their outer lives with the same degree of rigor, instead preferring to keep their options open as much as possible. It is not uncommon, therefore, for INTP to under-perform their often-substantial abilities, forgetting important appointments, procrastinating on projects and failing to recognize the emotional impact of their actions on themselves or others. However, mature INTP have overcome such trivial issues and combine their extensive exploratory tendencies with extraverted judgment that is strong enough to make INTP effective in the outer world. INTP can easily be distinguished from INTJ, who are far more structured in their outer lives while, inwardly, far more open-ended.

Fe plays a mildly unconscious, but significant role in INTP psychology. As noted above, INTP highly value precision in language, often pointing to the dictionary as evidence of a language crime. INTP readily acknowledge the inherent subjectivity of language because one's use of language cannot be separate from one's unique experience of it. INTP would, moreover, admit that some language is effective because it breaks the expected rules and norms. Yet, INTP nevertheless insist on precision. In this, one finds testimony of INTP's Fe use because it has already been shown that language can never be exact, only exact enough. Such insistence, therefore, must not be the result of logic, though there is a logic to language, but the result of INTP's value of effective communication, which demands words, terms and figures that are understood collectively. INTP tend to be most comfortable expressing their deductive insights when they know that those insights will be of value to their audience. That is why academia is so suited to INTP, who are often among the most demanding yet rewarding professors. Otherwise, they tend to live and let live, allowing all to bear the consequences, good or bad, of their own conclusions. Even though feeling is INTP's inferior function, INTP tend to be far warmer than TJ types, who introvert their feelings. INTP, therefore, tend to understand the social game a bit better than TJs, though the tradeoff is diminished understanding of their own motivations and feelings.

With Te as an unconscious function, INTP tend to have a love-hate relationship with rules, policies and laws—often believing their own understanding to be superior, though INTP recognize the necessity of such systems. What INTP disdain is being forced to give undue credence to a fact or figure, pointing out that a fact is only as useful as its context. Nevertheless, INTP show real facility using this function in short bursts. When forced to use this process habitually, however, INTP's trouble with Te quickly begins to show its face; and it is not uncommon to find INTP leaving out key steps in processes they might be designing, forgetting essential ingredients for a recipe or implementing a plan in the wrong order. There is a deductive logic to structuring the outer world effectively, just as the best deductive arguments make use of empirical insights. INTP's mastery of their thinking function goes to the next level when this link between introverted and extraverted thought becomes a part of their daily considerations. It would be a mistake to think that even mature INTP would be among the chief defenders of law and order, which INTP tend to regard with a degree of suspicion; it would be much more likely that INTP defend individuals' freedoms from excessive attempts to impose law and order. Se, however, is tougher for INTP, who tend to have limited awareness of their immediate environment, focusing instead on how the environment makes them feel. With Se as the function that INTP find most frustrating, it should hardly be surprising that INTP struggle not only to make concrete realities out of their visions and conclusions, but also struggle to see why such efforts are important in the first place. Fortunately, well-developed INTP have overcome this difficulty by working to make the world a better place for others in small, but significant ways.

When INTP's inner and outer psychologies are combined, one finds natural philosophers. Using Ti, INTP aim to understand the world and themselves according to their internal logical framework. Any data, whether emerging from within or without, is checked mercilessly for logical consistency; if any error were admitted into their frameworks, INTP feel their own demise would be imminent. INTP do not rely on the outer world to validate their views, they rely on their own deductive reasoning. While such a strategy lends INTP a quiet air of independence, it also means that admitting errors into INTP's frameworks is equivalent to building a house upon the sand. Once data has been validated and built into INTP's logical structure, it can safely be applied to the outer world in INTP's endless efforts to explore possibilities and gather new insights into the nature of reality and the meaning of life. Si helps lend INTP's reasoning a sense of constancy, for truth cannot change and, therefore, there is no need to retread old ground. It also helps limit INTP's theoretical exploration by ensuring that the exploration accords with INTP's everyday experience of the world. Fe gives INTP a sense of relatedness to their communities and a desire to advocate for the truth; it compels mature representatives of this type to philosophize about society's values, question the logic underlying various codes of ethics and operate from a perch that allows them to apply the ointment of truth to society's wounds.

INTP's judgments are highly polarized toward their dominant Ti and, thus, away from their inferior Fe. INTP are logicians at heart, and they will not allow value judgments of any sort to pollute their search for truth. It is not that INTP lack regard for values, for, as a general rule, one does not search for that which one does not value. Moreover, the belief that truth is best ascertained by deductive reasoning is merely a value, and that belief can only be considered logical given other value judgments; namely, truth obtained by means of deductive logic is better than truth obtained by sensation, feelings, empirical logic or intuition. Any mature INTP would acknowledge that deductive logic, while sometimes superior to other methods, is only one of several ways to arrive at truth. Despite INTP's preference for cold logic, they still desire warm and cordial relationships because, to this type, feelings, emotions and values belong to the group. With their feelings buried at the bottom of their psychic hierarchy, INTP are not at all dogmatic in their efforts to uphold the group's values, and this type only takes the collective's sense of ethics seriously insofar as the collective's morality allows enough room for the individual's search for truth. INTP's extraverted judgments sound immature and poorly considered in comparison to their introverted judgment—a natural consequence of this highly polarized relationship.

With Ti as the dominant function, Ne is not free to take too much of Si's libido for itself. INTP like to deal with the outer world in an exploratory way, always enquiring into possibilities and pondering the world not only with their deductive logic, but also by putting forth what-if questions. INTP leave their options open, avoid drawing premature conclusions and consider multiple points of view. This type enjoys intellectual novelty and abstract ideas. With Si right next door, INTP also value traditions, routine and stability. This type craves physical comfort and values history with the same intensity that ENTJ chase tangible results and promote concrete change. Because INTP, like ENTJ, use the intuition-sensation dichotomy with a minimal degree of polarization, INTP are not susceptible to many of the challenges that sometimes trip up Ne-dominant types; chief among those challenges is a propensity for entertaining unlikely possibilities. Such a tendency certainly gives Ne-dominant types creative flair, but it also means that these types sometimes have nothing to show for their efforts. INTP, on the other hand, are so insistent on using logical validity as their guiding principle that their ideational exploration is more likely to be delimited by previously drawn conclusions. Any ideas that emerge from their exploration are built into INTP's memory and inform future investigations.

ESFJ

FE	SI
NE	TI
FI	SE
NI	TE

ESFJ are oriented primarily to the outer world by means of Fe and, to a lesser extent, Ne. Se and Te operate outside of conscious awareness.

With Fe as ESFJ's dominant function, all other functions are necessarily subordinate to its demands.

Fe organizes the outer world, focusing on people and the values that unite them. In studying any group, one finds that though common goals do not always unite people, the emphasis or rejection of certain values makes each collective unique: Americans value freedom, liberty and justice; health-nuts value fresh produce and smoothies; workers value high wages and good benefits. Fe helps establish, regulate and update these collective values. Placing harmonious interactions above self-righteous stances, Fe does what is right for the present moment, whether that means building relationships, standing up for the afflicted or adjusting a moral stance to the unique needs of the situation. ESFJ, therefore, know how to make anyone feel at home, perfectly managing any event they are hosting down to the finest detail. ESFJ easily find what unites them to others and use that knowledge to find common ground. This type generally remains cordial even in the presence of those with whom its members disagree or dislike. Because Fe demands order in the outer world just as much as Te, strong Fe-types can be just as dogmatic as any Te-type. However, ESFJ tend to reserve any displays of indignation for those who have stepped on traditional moral fault lines, whereas Te-types tend to display their sharp tongues more readily.

ESFJ, on one hand, can be understood largely in terms of their dominant extraverted judgment, which drives them to seek closure and completion in the outer world with a degree of determination and constancy that can be awesome or awful, depending on one's point of view. For, just as Te's rule-making and policy-enforcement tendencies can be off-putting to those who value freedom and flexibility in their outer lives, Fe's insistence on managing the emotional ambiance and adherence to moral norms can be a source of frustration to those who believe that it is more important to be true to one's own feelings and inner moral compass. Fortunately, mature ESFJ can avoid this pitfall more often than not because they usually see several options or ways to get everyone on the same page.

With Ne as their preferred way of taking in information from the outside world, ESFJ enjoy exploration. Ne explores the world abstractly, asking what-if questions and doing everything in its power to keep its options open. Mature ESFJ tend to demonstrate substantial verbal fluidity and readily find the links between what has been and what could be. With its exploratory nature inextricably linked to the mental sphere, Ne does not focus directly on the physical world, but instead focuses on what things could become. This should hardly be surprising because possibilities are intangible by their very nature; e.g., it is possible cookie batter will become cookies, but cognizance of that possibility is not the result of objective sensory perception, nor could it be until the cookies are baked and the possibility takes on a physical reality. Moreover, that cookie batter can become cookies is a possibility relating to the world outside of oneself, thus the possibility is objective, despite its abstract nature.

ESFJ are recognized as one of the most observant types, but that powerful observation does not extend to the world of corporeal objects (Se). Indeed, ESFJ spend little time confronting physical reality exactly as it is, and instead focus their attention on the impact observable reality has on them (Si). ESFJ record the details of their internal sensory experience into their memories the way a stenographer records the details of a court proceeding. Because ESFJ are not prone to observing the outside world, remembering where they put their things can be a struggle for them. Despite ESFJ's unconscious use of Se, they still tend to show some competence using the function, especially when they want to criticize themselves or others, pointing to concrete examples of failures. Te, however, tends to be more challenging. With their focus on making the world a harmonious and congenial place, ESFJ can hardly see the point of Te's approach, which seems overly focused on the integrity of the system—sometimes to the detriment of the people for whom the system is meant to work. Many Te users would disagree with that characterization, and conflicts between Te and Fe's goals and priorities often lead to real-world tensions between strong Fe-types and strong Te-types.

ESFJ's introversion is most strongly characterized by Si and, to a lesser degree, Ti. Fi and Ni operate unconsciously. With Si as the auxiliary and lead introverted function, ESFJ are far more traditional and inwardly grounded than their ENFJ counterparts. Even though both types use Fe as their dominant function, the differences in their auxiliary and tertiary functions give the two types distinctly different flavors. Si gives ESFJ practicality, and because Si is the function most associated with memory, this type is unlikely to forget birthdays and anniversaries. Because the specifics of their physical lives are not somewhere outside of them, but deeply personal aspects of their human experience, ESFJ really get into the zone when handling detailed work like sewing, preparing gourmet meals or detailing a car. The internalized sensory experience, the incredible memories, the abiding desire to honor tradition, these all make ESFJ a comfort-seeking people — placing familiarity of experience above intensity of experience in nearly all cases and making for a type that hates the slightest sign of risk. Indeed, much of ESFJ's efforts at building social networks, offering a lending hand or entertaining guests are done, in part, to ingratiate themselves to their communities — trusting that they can rely on others in times of trouble because others have been able to rely on them. Moreover, because ESFJ prefer Si to its counterpart, Ne, they tend to be deeply skeptical of anything new — new colleagues, new toothpaste brands, new neighborhoods; and ESFJ will hardly tolerate the presence of anything new without subjecting it to the most rigorous tests. "Why change it if it's not broken?" an ESFJ might ask to prevent the establishment of a new system or policy. This type sometimes fears the possibility that change could bring catastrophe and often points out that the current system is at least predictable and reliable, despite its flaws.

ESFJ are also characterized by their inferior function, Ti. The inferior function is undifferentiated in all types, relegated to the most collective and rudimentary uses of the function, but influential nevertheless — a direct result of the inferior function's polar relationship with the dominant function. ESFJ, like ENFJ, are deeply attuned to the hidden rules, laws and definitions that govern effective communications and relationships, and this can be understood by strong Fe-types' consideration of chains of causation in relationships. "I could get Charlie that gift, but then Lucy might be upset since her birthday present wasn't as expensive, and if Lucy is upset, I'll have the whole family upset with me," an ESFJ might say. Ti helps ESFJ pick the right words at the right times and couch harsh criticism in the warmest of language. Members of this type can guide conversations in directions that allow them to paper over differences that might lead to conflict in favor of subjects where there is greater common interest. Because this function is undifferentiated in ESFJ, elaborate systems of logic that are unrelated to people and their values can appear daunting or even impenetrable. This is not to say ESFJ lack intellectual horsepower, for many tackle with ease logical systems about which they were trained or educated. Even ESFJ who are thoroughly versed on deductive logic will find Ti tiring when forced to use it for sustained periods. ESFJ tend to be more interested in practical understanding than theoretical pursuits because they prefer Si over Ti.

Because ESFJ use Fi unconsciously, they are not nearly as well in tune with their own feelings, values and ethical beliefs as they are the group's values; and it is to the group valuation that ESFJ defer, for as a Fe-type, the objective factor is decisive. Accordingly, ESFJ appear somewhat fickle in their appraisals to types who prefer Fi, seeming to place pleasing others ahead of authenticity to their own core beliefs. To strong Fi-types, such behavior must surely seem anathema, just as Fi's detachment from the group affect could be off-putting to strong Fe-types.

ESFJ still have some competence using Fi since, being the shadow of ESFJ's dominant function, it is so closely related to Fe. On the other hand, Ni is by far the most challenging function for ESFJ, who, more than any other type except ESTJ, really struggle to understand how meaning could be derived subjectively; to be fair, types who prefer the Se-Ni axis struggle to understand how one can have a subjective sensory experience. However, all people derive at least some meaning subjectively, and all have personalized, yet universal, sensations of the world. People simply prefer to experience the world one way or the other, and the opposing side is left no choice but to operate unconsciously. With sufficient reflection, however, one can catch glances of oneself using each function or, rather, being used in some cases; and it is exactly that kind of reflection that Ni makes possible, as it is the function that comes closest to perceiving the psyche itself.

When ESFJ's inner and outer personalities are combined, one finds natural event planners, hosts and hostesses. ESFJ are natural leaders focused on fostering bonds, establishing common values and setting the boundaries on acceptable behavior. Highly communicative, ESFJ love to check in with their friends and guests to make sure everyone is on the same page and having an enjoyable time. Directing the emotional atmosphere with certainty, ESFJ can be insistent about making sure everyone is displaying the right feelings, feelings that lead to an uplifting and joyous environment. ESFJ can be just as bossy as ESTJ, but instead of giving direct orders, ESFJ appeal to values and feelings, and the threat of social isolation is ever present for those who might not comply. Because this type is so in tune with routine, tradition and history, ESFJ instinctively know the right themes, colors and music to set a room's vibe.

With their highly internalized experience of the world and impeccable memories, no detail is small enough to elude ESFJ's eyes. Mature ESFJ clearly sense the possibilities and factor them into their plans. "My client invited 100 guests, but are we prepared if more show up?" an ESFJ might ask. ESFJ often have incredible verbal fluency, never at a loss for conversation topics or ways to turn a chat to their advantage. When it comes time for reflection, however, ESFJ are not as interested, much preferring action to examination, in contrast to ISFJ, who prefer to make sure they fully considered the consequences before they act.

ESFJ's judgments are polarized away from their inferior Ti and, therefore, towards their dominant Fe. ESFJ are firm and directive, though their directions are normally given with a smile. They love to give structure to the world, and they do it by managing feelings. ESFJ love to make other people feel good and love the social currency that comes with that talent. This type finds people who do not readily show or express their feelings a bit troubling, as it makes such people difficult to understand or manage. This is equivalent to ESTJ finding those who lack competence off-putting, believing such people undermine efficient, standardized operations. ESFJ believe feelings and values belong to groups and communities, so it is the collective who arbitrates between right and wrong, moral and immoral, not the individual. ESFJ are so quick to act that they sometimes regret their choices. ESFJ are great when everything is as it appears, but they sometimes struggle when they act or express their judgments before understanding all the logical nuances involved. If there is conflict, ESFJ generally try to get everyone on the same page by managing the emotional atmosphere before attempting to work through the causes of any emotional turbulence. ESFJ can get on with almost anybody by sharing feeling tones, but they sometimes struggle when the logic underlying another's values conflicts with ESFJ's own understanding—such as when interacting with someone from a much different culture.

On the other hand, there is far less polarization between ESFJ's auxiliary Si and tertiary Ne. Because Fe is the dominant player in the ESFJ psyche, Si is not free to steal much of the libido Ne needs to reach consciousness. ESFJ are in tune with their bodies and they are innately aware of how the world affects their physical state. They feel as if they carry their histories and traditions in their bones, so ESFJ think that in respecting their traditions and remembering their backgrounds, they are honoring their families, communities and, ultimately, themselves. Because of their internalized sense of the world, ESFJ not only have great memories for details, but also have a special talent for relating the present to the past. Though ESFJ do not have the same patience for analysis typically observed in ISFJ, many ESFJ still enjoy abstractions and are comfortable handling theoretical frameworks. This type tends to be more comfortable thinking about the future than Si-dominant types since mature ESFJ do not see the future as something to be feared, but as a natural part of life.

ENTP

NE	TI
FE	SI
NI	TE
FI	SE

ENTP are oriented primarily to the outer world by Ne and, to a lesser extent, Fe. Te and Se operate unconsciously.

With Ne as the dominant function, every other function is subordinate to its dictates.

Ne naturally perceives the objective possibilities inherent in subjective sensory phenomena. In this way, Ne-dominant types bear a strong resemblance to Si-dominant types. However, Ne — especially in the dominant position — suppresses subjective sensory stimuli, thus allowing Ne's exploration of objective possibilities to flow freely. With their perceptions so structured, ENTP are wizards of potentialities, never lacking ideas for what this or that might become, even if such ideas seem to cultivate the angel of the bizarre. No matter how strange or foreign such ideas might seem, ENTP's perceptions always bear a clear and definite relation to the objective situation. Yes, it is quite unlikely that a fire truck would become a house, but it certainly could. In this way, Ne-dominants are the Rorschach ink-blotters of the psychological types, looking at inkblot after inkblot and determining from their own subjective sense what potentials exist in the blots. "I see a candle. No, two old women," ENTP might say in an attempt to associate an objective meaning with their subjective sense of the inkblot.

ENTP are not able to follow every possibility to its conclusion and, therefore, ENTP need some way to determine what possibilities are most deserving of their efforts, time and examination. Every possibility, association or potentiality is, therefore, infused with an evaluation of the idea's objective value. Fe, sharing the same extraverted attitude as the dominant function, helps to limit, even mildly, ENTP's exploration to ideas that are collectively valued — whether that valuation comes from home, school, the community or society at large. This combination of Ne and Fe can even cause ENTP to appear like a feeling type to those who are not well versed in typology since the combination of these two functions means that ENTP are deeply interested in possibilities related to people; and accordingly, ENTP have many of the tools needed to dominate the social scene.

With Fe as the lead extraverted judging function, ENTP's judgments regarding the outer world are voiced primarily through Fe. Therefore, ENTP typically sound soft and weak in their extraverted judgments even when the internal judgments, which receive priority in the ENTP psyche, are final. ENTP, thus, appear to be more compassionate, supportive, and committed to societal values and norms than their inner psychology would indicate. This is the exact opposite of what is seen in INTJ, who are far more in touch with their feelings and values than their cold, unfeeling appearance would show. That is not to say that ENTP have few or no strongly held values, but ENTP tend to be adamant about society's most axiomatic principles, paying just enough lip service to those values deemed less important to ingratiate themselves to those whose support is needed or desired. Despite their dominant Ne, ENTP tend to make value judgments that are rather black and white, which is to be expected given the comparatively limited scope the tertiary function holds in the psyche.

Even though Te is unconscious in this type, ENTP are comfortable enough with facts, figures, rules and regulations, and when needed, ENTP are more than capable of designing and implementing the steps needed to get from Point A to Point B. However, ENTP's Te tends to emerge most often for criticism, both of themselves and others. At those times, ENTP can be quite ENTJ-like in their ability to expose sequential lapses, failures to follow policy, or improper use of facts and data; consistently expecting ENTP to live up to such criticism, themselves, can be a harrowing task. While such criticism is delivered via Te, the heart of the matter often lies with a violation of a closely held collective value. ENTP use of Se is quite limited. Accordingly, ENTP show only the most rudimentary awareness of the objective, physical world — often failing to see things right in front of them or failing to notice that their car keys were moved. With Se in this humble position, ENTP's hunt for possibilities does not extend to the physical world, where ENTP struggle to take immediate, concrete action even in service of the possibilities most desired.

ENTP's inner psychology is most strongly characterized by Ti and, to a lesser degree, Si. Ni and Fi are used unconsciously. With Ti as the lead introverted function, ENTP are quite adept at systematizing, categorizing and forming valid logical deductions. The people who know ENTP best are familiar with this type's ability to split even the finest hair. Of course, ENTP would not be so heartless as to demonstrate this habit all the time because ENTP prefer open-ended exploration; but when ENTP are frustrated, this hairsplitting habit rears its head. Nevertheless, Ti gives the ENTP personality a sense of gravity that would otherwise be lacking. Ti is especially important for ENTP since their dominant function, Ne, is more than capable of offering innumerable possibilities but is incapable of arriving at any estimation of the possibilities' chances of becoming reality. Ti is needed, therefore, to figure out which possibilities are most or least likely to manifest. Like their INTJ cousins, ENTP are conscious of the widest field of information possible since their psyche is structured in a top-down fashion, with Ne followed by Ti, Fe and Si respectively.

It would be inaccurate, however, to claim that ENTP or INTJ are the most conscious among the types since many intricate details are overlooked in their big-picture outlook on life. Consequently, Si is of the utmost importance to ENTP's psychic equilibrium because Si is not only ENTP's primary way of getting hold of details, it puts a check on Ne's exploratory tendencies by limiting the field of data under consideration to objective possibilities emerging from long-established data points. In other words, Si prevents Ne from going off the rails by ensuring that the possibilities bear clear relation to hands-on experience and tradition. All people have world views, but with a dominant function that explores what might be, ENTP are not able to rely on their Ne to complete that point of view; indeed, to the extent ENTP have a stable worldview, it is often to remain open-minded. Therefore, Ti explicates the logical principles underlying the possibilities' connections to the Si starting point, and once those principles have been thoroughly understood and their universal validity ascertained, ENTP incorporate those principles into their Si map of the world. When later confronted with familiar sensations, ENTP will not only have a clear feeling of the sensation and its effect on them, but also the logical deductions that previously accompanied those sensations. While ENTP typically display only a superficial awareness of their environment, ENTP's inner sensory experience is not only more conscious, but also richer than their sense of the outer world. One, then, will rarely hear ENTP speak of physical reality as it is; exploration of *what is* interests ENTP little compared to exploring *what could be*. In describing their sensory experience, expect ENTP to focus almost exclusively on what the world is like to themselves. That their individual sensory experience might comport little with others' experience rarely reaches ENTP consciousness since the data that comprises subjective, sensory experience nevertheless leads to this type finding worthwhile possibilities to explore — no matter how strange the starting point might have been.

ENTP are not only deft at finding the objective possibilities that emerge from subjective sensory experience but have some degree of facility in discovering the individual, subjective meaning inherent in any objective experience of the concrete world. However, with Ni being such a subtle function, ENTP are not at all likely to realize just how often they use it. A person named Kelly walking down the street has a physical reality that cannot be denied, yet Kelly's meaning is not only able to be understood objectively in terms of possibilities, but also subjectively in terms of meaning. To one person, for example, Kelly is mom, and to another, Kelly is an executive, and to yet another, a best friend. Though such an example displays only a rudimentary usage of Ni, it does illustrate just how large a role Ni plays in everyone's life. To be fair, the same data can be interpreted through the Si-Ne prism, as should be obvious since people often arrive at similar conclusions despite differing psychologies. Fi, on the other hand, is a far more sensitive subject for ENTP, who are profoundly unaware of just how much their subjective values and feelings affect not only themselves, but also others; and with their typically black-and-white application of Fe, ENTP are not much willing to tolerate Fi displays, especially of the negative variety. However, ENTP would do well to remember that a valuation that puts collective values above individual values is, in reality, a Fi value directed toward Fe concerns—a good reminder of the fundamental unity of each factor of consciousness, whether the factor is introverted or extraverted.

When ENTP's outer and inner personalities are combined, one finds a type with incredible entrepreneurial talent. No type is better at hunting down opportunities and crafting plans designed to capitalize on as many of their prospects as possible. In this way, ENTP differ mildly from their shadow type, INTJ, because INTJ organize all their efforts toward achieving an overarching vision. Therefore, INTJ are stronger at crafting strategies all but guaranteed to achieve the desired result. ENTP, on the contrary, work to position themselves to capitalize on the opportunities that emerge from their free-flowing exploration. One can see this in how even the most mature ENTP get bored with following through on many of their projects, ceasing all effort once things get dull. Ne tells the ENTP about the objective possibilities, always enquiring how this can become that. Ti limits those possibilities by discarding the ones that are logically invalid. Unlike INTJ's Te, however, ENTP's Ti does not deal with certitudes in the outer world, but probabilities. There is a 50 percent chance that the light is on in the next room; if the company employs this growth strategy, there is a 75 percent chance that overall revenue will increase by 20 percent, despite a 90 percent chance of decreased sales in three major markets. In this way, ENTP are also capable strategists because ENTP's strategies seek to leave open as many roads to success as possible. INTJ, however, might eliminate positive opportunities in service of single-mindedly realizing, even guaranteeing, their vision. When mature, ENTP tend to be charming and sincere owing to their tertiary Fe, and when combined with Si, ENTP generally feel compelled to make real efforts to gain acceptance by adhering to traditional rules and norms—again, this is assuming a fair amount of development.

ENTP's perceptions are quite polarized away from their inferior Si and, therefore, towards their dominant Ne. This polarization is nothing terrible because the polarization between the dominant function and the inferior fuels the individuation process—the dominant function siphons off libido from the inferior, an act needed for the dominant's differentiation. Unfortunately, ENTP are prone to relishing in this polarization, a potential problem that is in no way limited to this type. Should ENTP fail to make sufficient room for their inferior Si's insights, however, ENTP will find that their dominant Ne begins to consider possibilities and options that are not plausible since Si delimits the possibilities under consideration using experience. In such cases, ENTP lose their clear sense of the possibilities because ENTP have lost their sense of the history. A single, subjective data point emerging from Si could be explored in countless ways, but since Si is a comprehensive — that is, universal—map of sensory experience, ENTP are steadied by the fact that their objective explorations must account for broad swaths of their real-world experience. It is not necessary that ENTP make inferior Si their governing principle. However, just as INTJ are best served by making sure their dominant Ni meshes with Se reality, ENTP are happiest when they ensure that Ne's insights correspond with Si data. In so doing, ENTP can significantly increase the scope of their consciousness.

There is far less polarization between ENTP's auxiliary Ti and tertiary Fe—a natural consequence of the fact that the auxiliary function, though fairly well differentiated, is not free to use up libido to the same degree that the dominant function is. Consequently, it is hard not to be struck by the power of a well-developed ENTP's Fe, even though the tertiary function typically shows little, if any, differentiation. ENTP primarily use Ti to form judgments, but since Ti is in the introverted attitude, such judgments generally relate to themselves or are, otherwise, kept private. The judging side most of the world sees is ENTP's somewhat naïve need to connect with others, be liked and uphold, though weakly, social norms—naïve not because Fe usage is such, but because of the simple, yet earnest way ENTP tend to use Fe. Naiveté notwithstanding, ENTP's entrepreneurial skills are enhanced by their ability to ingratiate themselves to their audience. INTJ are characteristically described as unemotional robots. By observing the striking power of ENTP's tertiary feeling, however, one can really begin to understand how powerful a role INTJ's tertiary Fi must have in their psychic landscape.

Psychology of Se-Ni, Fe-Ti Types

ISTP

TI	SE
NI	FE
TE	SI
NE	FI

ISTP are largely oriented to their inner worlds through their dominant function Ti and, to a lesser extent, their tertiary function, Ni. ISTP also use Si and Fi, though their use is largely unconscious.

With Ti as the dominant function, every other function is necessarily subordinate to Ti's dictates.

Ti structures information in logical ways. Where Te simply seeks an understanding that is complete enough for the task at hand, Ti seeks an understanding that is comprehensive and, therefore, universally applicable. Ti immediately and ruthlessly eliminates assertions that are deemed illogical and always checks for consistency. Setting the attainment of truth above all other aims, Ti constantly works to discover underlying relationships, instinctively noting that there is an effect for every cause and a cause for every effect. Though easy going by nature, ISTP can be distinguished from INTP by ISTP's orientation to physical reality. Where the INTP is happy to explore causality abstractly, ISTP naturally grasp causality in the real world; learning how an engine works simply by observing how one part affects another, and the circumstances in which that effect can or cannot be reproduced; producing beautiful pieces of furniture by studying construction techniques, experimenting with their craft and building their practical insights into their logical construct; making the perfect steak every time, not because ISTP relied on a cooking class, but because of an almost scientific sort of trial and error. One word that aptly describes ISTP is independence. ISTP believe that they are the ones best qualified to manage their comings and goings, their methods of operation, their manners of being — for these are subjects about which ISTP have thought deeply. That is not to say that others will be pleased with ISTP's methods, for there can be a tendency to set oneself above others simply due to introverted judgment's ascendancy in ISTP's psychology. So, despite ISTP's high level of psychic organization, it is not at all uncommon for them to struggle with managing the outer world, often struggling with basics like punctuality.

Another distinction between ISTP and INTP is that the former are far less rigid in their internal psychic structure. Because they use tertiary Ni, not tertiary Si, ISTP show much less concern with maintaining familiar patterns of thought or psychic organization than they do integrating unconscious contents and observing psychic patterns. This distinction tends to result in ISTP believing that many truths cannot be explained, only lived, while INTP are more likely to subject those truths to the most rigorous analysis.

This is because Ni naturally gets a look behind the curtain, picking up on psychological data that eludes some types. Keeping in mind that all opposites must balance, it should be clear ISTP do not need to be as rigid in their internal structure as INTP because ISTP do not apply their logical insights abstractly, but concretely — freeing the ISTP to follow fluidly Ni's archetypal insights internally. If one were to imagine a cone, Se is the point at the cone's apex and Ni would be the round base, constituting an information field that holds the Se data point within. Though ISTP are far more aware of the cone's apex or the objective data point — take a car, for example — ISTP are also sufficiently aware of the subjective field of information in which the data point is held. Therefore, the data point's past and future, the hidden implications and suppositions attached to such a data point are matters to which mature ISTP give attention. For example, a car implies its driver, a manufacturer, streets and highways, good music or fun road trips. Lacking such a subjective field, it would be impossible to have any understanding of the physical world. Consequently, mature ISTP often just know where a situation is heading, deftly maneuvering to best position themselves for the outcome they want. Ni makes it possible for ISTP to use insights they gathered working on their old beater to overhaul an engine in another model — easily spotting the patterns that applied in both cases and exploiting that knowledge to make a real-world impact.

ISTP use Si in a characteristically unconscious fashion, but that does not mean that they are unskilled in its use. Because Si comports with their dominant function's point of view, Si does receive a sliver of ISTP's attention. Its use tends to be reserved for criticism of themselves or others, and it usually comes to the fore when tertiary Ni has had enough. At such times, ISTP are quick to point to incompetence handling detailed or intricate work, like accounting or sewing. They point out failures to adhere to long-held traditions and norms and rely more on their subjective sense of events (Si) than their typical objective style (Se), which generally compels ISTP to adjust to the tangible situation. Fi, however, is a far more difficult topic for ISTP, who are profoundly out of touch with their unique motivations, morality and values. Because Fi is highly antagonistic to ISTP's preferred mode of operation, they find it much easier to stick to working things out logically or, otherwise, going with the flow and deriving their moral standards from their communities.

ISTP's outer psychology consists of Se and Fe, while Te and Ne operate unconsciously. With Se as the lead extraverted function, ISTP are highly observant of the outer world; they spot practical opportunities and exploit them in service of a concrete result. Dealing with life just as it is, ISTP do not get too caught up with planning the details of their lives, preferring to go with the flow and handling challenges only once they have emerged, not a moment sooner. In this regard, Se and Ne could not be more different. Though both functions deal with the world in an open-ended way, Ne is concerned with what a thing might or might not become, while Se considers only what a thing is without labels, definitions or any data imposed onto it; i.e., Se concretely considers objective actualities while Ne abstractly works through objective potentials. When pure Se looks at a sheet of paper, it sees only the paper and might go on to consider its objective nature — its width, height, color, etc. Ne, however, merely begins its exploration with what is suggested by the paper — a tree or the manufacturing process. Ne might consider the paper's future — maybe it will be medium for artistic expression, or a shopping list, or maybe it will go straight to the landfill. None of those possibilities are observable by means of the five senses as long as they remain simple potentials. Pure Se, therefore, would remain completely unaware of those potentials. For its part, pure Ne would have no consciousness of the sheet paper from which its sense of those possibilities emerged. It should be clear, then, how essential Ni is to Se's success just as Si is needed to fill in the gaps that are missing in Ne's considerations.

Because it directly opposes their dominant function, ISTP's inferior Fe plays a significant, though somewhat unconscious, role in their psychology. ISTP spend most of their time defining, categorizing and breaking down their experiences into a logical construct. This type spends relatively little time addressing value systems and emotions directly. One can only fully connect to a communal value system if one has a sense of the subjective logic that underlies it. Thus, it seems cruel that as one of the two types with the clearest sense of that subjective logical structure, ISTP have little interest in directly exploring or participating in collective systems of valuation, instead incorporating root communal values like effective communication, equitable behavior and ethics into ISTP's framework as the very roots of their logical deliberations. Nevertheless, Fe's humble role in ISTP's psychology is enough to compel this type to seek out harmonious relationships and groups of like-minded people, who not only provide ISTP with much needed emotional support but compel ISTP to spend at least some of their time applying their unique logical insights to the outer world in the form of collective values. ISTP, of course, return the favor by helping others to apply their values in logically consistent ways.

Though ISTP are very strong logicians, they tend to be hit-or-miss with structuring their extraverted lives and the outer world. That is because ISTP like to use logic to structure their inner world; and because their primary extraverted judging function occupies the inferior role, ISTP are quite free-flowing in their outer lives. With ISTP limiting their inferior extraverted judgment to the most rudimentary and essential elements, it should not be shocking that ISTP prefer not to use Te — its rules, its policies and standardization — any more than is necessary. Not only is Te antagonistic to this type's preferred manner of structuring the outer world (Fe), Te can put the brakes on Se's free-flowing exploration with immediacy, placing schedules and productivity standards far above Se-types' preference for dealing with life as it comes. One of the struggles that types with weak Te tend to encounter — namely, an inability to deal with facts and hard data — is no challenge for ISTP because Se directs this type to a deeply realistic and fact-based view of the outer world. Ne, however, is far more of an annoyance. Strong Ne-types' tendency to deal with the outer world not as it is, but as it could be, quickly gets old for ISTP, who believe that such speculation is a waste of time.

When ISTP's inner and outer psychologies are combined, one finds the world's natural craftsmen, mechanics and builders. Ti allows ISTP to build a logical model; this framework is always internal, and any empirical facts only serve to inform its speculation, not direct it. In distinction to Te, which minimizes deductive considerations in favor of results, Ti will not proceed until it completely understands the consequences of its choices — a good thing because it takes much more effort for Ti to remove error from its model than Te, whose framework is empirical and, therefore, changes as more facts emerge. Ti, on the other hand, seeks to reach an understanding so deep that it need not rely on facts. Se attunes ISTP to tangible reality and compels them to direct their logical prowess to concrete phenomena, and it is this powerful combination of Ti and Se that makes ISTP wizards of concrete systems. ISTP are just as capable as any other type at directing their logic towards abstractions, but it is not their passion. Ni helps ISTP to determine what is hidden, it helps them identify cause and effect that cannot be seen with their eyes, and because ISTP use this Ti-Ni one-two punch to eliminate causes for problems in a system (like plumbing, for example), it makes them master troubleshooters. Fe propels ISTP, who are so inclined to quiet observation, to concrete action, compelling ISTP to apply their judgments to the outer world in the form of statements or, more likely, actions that reflect their values.

ISTP's judgments are highly polarized away from their inferior Fe and, therefore, toward their dominant Ti. ISTP are logicians at heart. Inwardly decisive and firm, members of this type are not as imposing in their outer presentation. While INTP love to nitpick word choice and other abstract considerations to no end, ISTP are just as brutal in their quibbles over concrete considerations. "Why would John build a motor that way?" an ISTP might wonder to herself. "Not only is fuel going to cost him a fortune, but the engine is likely to overheat." ISTP uncover logical principles when they reflect on their real-world experiences and observations. Because ISTP express their judgments about the outer world through their inferior function, their judgments tend to sound weak and ineffectual in comparison to the often-significant force ISTP are prepared to bring to bear in executing their judgments. As a result, ISTP are much more confident simply demonstrating their conclusions than voicing them, viewing their actions as sufficient expression of their feelings. Because Ti thoroughly understands the logic and principles behind the social game, ISTP tend to treat social life as just that: a game. ISTP tend to believe that most people are too dogmatic about values and find Fe a bit silly and overly dramatic, at times.

ISTP show far less polarization between their auxiliary Se and tertiary Ni. Ti puts a sharp limit on Se's ability to rob libido from Ni and, thus, both Se and Ni have enough room to reach consciousness. Se makes ISTP highly observant and they are deeply in tune with their environment, catching the smallest motions, changes of tone or the subtlest flavors of a gourmet dish. Compared to ESTP, this type can seem sluggish or lazy, but when ISTP do take action, their results are dependable because they have taken the time to comprehend the world around them. ESTP are certainly more inclined to action, but that very inclination lends their results something of a haphazard nature in comparison to the ISTP's. Ni operates much more consciously in ISTP than in ESTP. Mature ISTP easily pick up on missing or hidden data because Ni looks beyond the obvious. Picking up on the missing clues, this type then re-engages Se in effort to fill in the blanks. ISTP generally know and understand far more than their words or, even activities, might indicate. They feel little of the need to show off or be the center of attention that is often observed in Se-dominant types.

INFJ

NI	FE
TI	SE
NE	FI
TE	SI

INFJ are oriented primarily to their inner worlds through their dominant function Ni and, to a lesser extent, their tertiary function, Ti. Si and Fi work unconsciously.

With Ni as the dominant function, every other function is necessarily subordinate to its demands.

Ni perceives the background processes of consciousness, including unconscious processes. Ni's function in the psyche could be compared with Hermes, the messenger of the gods, whose winged feet testify to the swiftness of his delivery. Life consists of a never-ending motion of unconscious contents into consciousness and, in turn, conscious contents into the unconscious. Every person possesses some awareness of this process, no matter how dim, and this can be evidenced by the universal tendencies of humanity to both learn and forget. Learning, obviously enough, is the process by which information of which one is unconscious comes to consciousness and forgetting is the process by which information of which one was once conscious becomes unconscious. Ni, in both theory and practice, allows all people to observe this process in symbolic form and, thus, acts as a kind of Hermes in the psyche by facilitating these processes.

Hence, INFJ and INTJ, as the two types with front-row seats for this ceaseless motion, tend to be viewed as almost psychic. Nevertheless, it is inaccurate to call Ni-dominants psychics or prophets. It is better to say that these types have skill in dealing with psychic processes, much in the same way that Se-dominants have singular talent for navigating tangible reality.

Time is a finite resource and, thus, INFJ are in no position to test or act upon all their observations of the psyche's seemingly infinite space; and while INFJ are outwardly far more caring, approachable and friendly than their INTJ cousins, that greater ability to extravert their feelings means that INFJ's ability to achieve logical consistency is a challenge, though a challenge that well-developed INFJ are more than equipped to handle. INFJ use Ti to define, categorize and refine their Ni insights. Just as INTJ use their tertiary Fi to determine which, if any, judgments, conclusions and actions are most important to achieving their vision, INFJ rely on Ti to ascertain the logical rules and root assumptions at work in their visions.

Ti is the function most prone to hairsplitting, and even though Ti is not associated with the ego block in INFJ, the hairsplitting still plays a significant role. It is not uncommon, therefore, for INFJ to work quietly at clarifying terms, developing frameworks and explicating causation. However, INFJ are quite the perfectionistic type when it comes to the products they will allow the outer world to see, only rivaled, in general, by INTJ. Therefore, INFJ keep much of their logical analysis to themselves in much the same way that INTJ keep their feelings to themselves. This perfectionistic tendency naturally results from dominant Ni, which often offers visions, goals and dreams that are more perfect than can ever be realized in observable reality. Thus, INFJ face the constant struggle between accepting only results that perfectly accord with their inner vision or, otherwise, allowing an imperfect result out of the belief that half the pie is better than none.

With it operating unconsciously, INFJ's primary use of Fi is to criticize themselves or others. It is, therefore, uncommon for INFJ to demonstrate the same profound awareness of their own feelings as they do of others'. INFJ can get a better sense of this dynamic by observing INTJ's use of Ti, which occupies the same place in the INTJ psyche as Fi does in INFJ's. INTJ are deeply aware of consensus views, opposing rationales and expert opinions, and INTJ deftly manipulate such to their ends. Ask INTJ what they, themselves, think and one finds that INTJ have given little consideration to their subjective reasoning, unless the topic is of importance (Fi) to them. INFJ, likewise, give little consideration to their subjective feelings and motivations unless the logical framework underpinning Fe's considerations demands it. Thus, while INFJ are often regarded as the natural psychologists among the types, it takes a good deal of development for those psychological insights to be applied to INFJ themselves and, therefore, INTJ often have superior insights into their own root motivations, while INFJ typically show more awareness of their root logical assumptions. INFJ's unconscious Si shows itself as poor body awareness, a disregard for traditions, a choice not to rely on routine to navigate the world and a struggle to keep track of minor sensory details.

INFJ's outer personality consists of Fe and Se, while Ne and Te operate unconsciously. With Fe as the lead extraverted function, INFJ are socially adept. Unlike ExFJ, who filter all incoming information through dominant Fe, INFJ use Fe to give their vision a reality (Se) and, therefore, Fe is an instrument in INFJ's hands, not their psyche's animating force. Fe is the instrument by which collective values are ascertained, established, and modified; by Fe one can either be made to feel like a welcomed part of the group or an irredeemable outcast; always meeting the needs of any person or moment with the appropriate feeling tones, Fe is ready to sacrifice for those who deserve it or scorn those whose errors are inexcusable. With Ni's famous detachment looming large in the INFJ's psychology, however, a careful observer gets the sense that INFJ are dispensing Fe in quite a calculated way, no matter how sincere the INFJ might be. One does not get the same sense from ISFJ, the only other type to use Fe in the auxiliary position, perhaps because their dominant function, Si, demands that Fe be used and applied in far more traditional ways—a compulsion that affects INFJ little.

Like other dominant intuitives, especially introverted intuitives, INFJ want to make concrete changes to the observable world, but with Se as the inferior function, INFJ's ability to make real-world change is precarious. Se allows one to make sense of the observable world. Without Se, one would not know that the sky is blue, or the feeling of sunshine; one would not even be able to eat. Though all those examples of Se usage are quite basic, they go a long way to show how foundational Se is to the ability to function in the world. On one hand, INFJ are uniquely situated to piece together the timeless nature of collective values, quickly sorting into two groups those values that are essential to successful civilizations and cultures, and the values that are mere symptoms of those civilizations. Ni allows INFJ to find archetypal patterns at work in all collectives. Fe makes it possible to understand the importance of values to distinct cultures and Ti compels INFJ to categorize those values in a consistent, logical manner. Bringing concrete change to society's applications of its values, on the other hand, requires INFJ to be mature because change does not come simply by analysis, but by real-world effort (Se). Achieving the desired changes also requires the ability to accept incremental or incomplete results because all real-world results must occur within the realm of time, and the basic laws of physics are quite clear that, at the macroscopic level, even the biggest, most sudden changes happen in increments. Thus, no essential step can be overlooked or cast aside in bringing about concrete change. Otherwise, not only could INFJ fail to bring about their desired result, adverse results might instead come to pass.

With Ne as an unconscious function, INFJ have some trouble with spontaneity. INFJ are better able to cope with that flaw than INTJ because INFJ have better interpersonal skills in the first place. Nevertheless, INFJ struggle to voice multiple possibilities without sufficient time for reflection, which is the natural consequence of a dominant function that seeks to find *the* possibility, not several plausible possibilities. Te, however, is more of a challenge for INFJ. Consider INTJ's Fe, which occupies the corresponding position in their psychic hierarchy as Te does in INFJ's. INTJ are typically characterized as unemotional robots even though mature INTJ are, inwardly, quite aware of their feelings; that is due to INTJ eschewing Fe in favor of Te. Since a strong Fe focus often serves to destabilize Te systems, INTJ's reticence to engage with Fe can hardly be shocking. Similarly, giving a lot of attention to Te rules, systems and laws keeps INFJ from focusing on what they are much more passionate about: people, culture and the values that both give rise to culture and that emerge because of it. A more systematic (Te) approach to life, INFJ would argue, keeps one from understanding and meeting the emotional needs of individuals. More importantly, Te is prone to treating culture and collective values as mere inconveniences that must be overcome to reach a goal, and to INFJ, such treatment must seem morally questionable. INTJ might respond that systems are collective rules meant to serve everyone, so too much focus on any individual's needs or wants quickly serves to undermine the system's effectiveness for all who are involved. INFJ, however, would argue that a system is flawed if it fails to incorporate society's values.

When INFJ's inner and outer personalities are combined, one finds the type with the best insight into society's values, beliefs and culture. More importantly, one sees a type not only committed to upholding those values, but also challenging the validity of values that have gone out of date. As a result, no other type is as important in providing the intellectual basis for the values most cherished by a community or organization. While INFJ are not quite as apt as ENFJ to fight to make change an everyday reality, INFJ's importance in the process can in no way be diminished. Of the four types with Fe in the dominant or auxiliary position, INFJ come across as the coldest and most detached. That is not because INFJ are any less caring than the others, but because of Ni's impersonal nature, which allows INFJ to detach from their own subjective point of view and see themselves as objects of perception. Ni-dominant types can view themselves through another's eyes, and because everyone uses Ni, everyone can have this experience. Jung wrote, "The subjective 'I live' becomes the objective 'It lives me.'"[32] These types naturally realize people never truly observe their environment, merely their own perceptions of the environment; and the mature ones recognize that one can never truly be separate from the environment that one is observing, for an observer cannot observe an environment in which he does not participate—at least on a mental level. The sensations, thoughts, feelings and intuitions all people experience attest to this participation. On some level, therefore, Ni disregards the abstraction of the observer versus the observed, objective versus subjective, and recognizes these abstractions as two sides of one experience. Therefore, Ni-dominant types tend to view excessive attempts at objectivity as deeply misguided, arguing that one can never be truly objective, only objective enough. Though such a formulation is necessarily paradoxical, people with well-developed Ni will find that it is nonetheless correct. Just because one can detach from one's own point of view does not mean that one is freed from the subjective aspect of perception, for there are no perceptions without a perceiver; i.e., subject. To view oneself through another's eyes requires one to become that other, in a psychological sense; and because INFJ also use Fe, the ability to assume another's view is the INFJ's specialty.

INFJ's perceptions are highly polarized toward their intuition and, therefore, away from their sensation. As a Ni-dominant type, INFJ often draw accurate conclusions from minimal data, even in cases when their primary data points come from their imaginations. That is because Ni is great at connecting the dots in such a way that the data tell a coherent story. This ability quickly becomes a limitation when that intuitive ability is not combined with appropriate Se usage. INFJ who are unable or unwilling to use Se would often draw incorrect conclusions simply because their intuition did not have the right data. Such people might conclude that a coworker is going to be fired because the coworker has been visibly stressed and overlooking parts of the job for which the coworker had been responsible. Now, the manager and HR representative just asked the coworker into the office for a meeting. However, the INFJ did not realize that the manager had been preparing the coworker for promotion for several months and had reassigned many of the coworker's responsibilities for the sake of developing the coworker for a new role. In this case, the INFJ had good reason to draw the initial conclusion, but the failure to notice and consider relevant data meant that the INFJ was wrong. INFJ who have integrated their inferior Se to a sufficient degree will not be prone to such errors. To be fair, that example is basic, and the average Ni-dominant person would have picked up on the missing data. The example is illustrative, however, of the pitfalls that can emerge from this highly polarized dichotomy.

INFJ's judgments are far less polarized and differentiated than their perceptions. As a result, INFJ shift between their Fe and Ti judgments with relative fluidity, which is another reason INFJ are uniquely qualified to teach society about its values. Since Fe holds a degree of ascendancy over Ti in INFJ, they are highly attuned to the joys and plights of those who encounter them, though perhaps not as much as their ENFJ counterparts. On the other hand, INFJ tend to show more awareness of the logical principles, categories and definitions that underpin this type's value judgments because Ti operates only one door over from its companion, Fe. Thus, INFJ's greatest contribution is their unique ability challenge society's application of its values, not by being the primary fighter for change, but by being the type most attuned to the logical discrepancy between collective values and the failure to live up to them.

ESTP

SE	TI
FE	NI
SI	TE
FI	NE

ESTP are chiefly oriented toward the outer world, and that orientation is governed by Se and, to a lesser extent, Fe. Ne and Te operate unconsciously.

Because ESTP use Se in the dominant position, every other function's use is directed and limited by Se.

Se is intensely aware of the outer world and, when it is the dominant function, it views the world in ultra-high definition. Capable of registering every detail of its environment with ease, Se notices the slightest movements, changes of facial expression, subtleties of tone and elusive notes of a fine perfume. With such adaptations to the outer world, ESTP do not focus their time on planning, thinking or reflecting, but deal with life at the moment, readily making use of the tools in their physical space. ESTP tend to be far more driven to action than ISTP since Se is ISTP's auxiliary function and, thus, ESTP spend much more time interacting with or, otherwise, dominating their environment. On the other hand, ISTP are far more inclined to think about their environment, internalize the outer world and the rules of the game, and step in to push the right button at the right time. ESTP, however, push buttons first and then note the reaction. They chide those who are too aloof with good-natured jokes and liven up a boring environment with enjoyable conversation. This type not only sports the latest styles, but also pushes fashion into new frontiers with daring new combinations of attire. Like Ne, which is largely driven by the intensity of an impulse, Se seeks the strongest sensory stimulus and, as a result, ESTP are prone to taking risks—trying foods that would scare off most others, learning the most difficult skateboard tricks or undertaking a high-risk, high-reward stance in a business negotiation.

One of the reasons ESTP can dominate their environment with such ease is due to their deep, but slightly underdeveloped, sense of community. ESTP have a profound desire to be liked and respected, and much of their behavior, attitude and disposition are directly driven by this craving. To be liked implies relationships, and it is these that ESTP use to conquer their environment.

This is because of ESTP's tertiary Fe, which compels this type to get in touch with and adhere to group values. Fe also gets a workout because it is ESTP's primary way of structuring the world and expressing their judgments to others. Mature ESTP, therefore, can be warm and friendly, using their sense of institutional or community values to bring the outer world into conformity with their will. No wonder Keirsey thought ESTP were natural sellers; and because mature ESTP have taken the time to build healthy relationships with others, they are able to get concrete support when they need it. Despite the fact that ESFP are far more conscious of their feelings than ESTP, it is not ESFP, but ESTP who come off as more charming and personable. That is because, unlike ESTP, ESFP do not extravert their feelings, they introvert them. ESFP instead show the outer world a sterner voice, Te, which has enough power in ESFP's tertiary position for its rule-making tendencies and policy-following habits to get noticed. This difference between ESTP and ESFP's tertiary function is the simplest way to tell apart these two types, who seem quite similar at first glance.

ESTP tend to treat Te as something of a battering ram, only bringing it out when pushed to the edge. At those times, Te is used as a brutal instrument of criticism, whether the criticism is directed at themselves or others. When this happens, ESTP are quick to point out procedural absurdities, factual inaccuracies and policy infractions. Because it is strongly opposed to their tertiary Fe, ESTP make little use of Te when it comes to ordering their outer lives. At times, ESTP can view Te as rather shallow because it does not function deductively, but empirically. Nevertheless, ESTP do not hesitate to rely on expert opinion and analysis when it supports the criticism they deliver. Ne, on the other hand, challenges this type to a far greater extent since Ne is the function most strongly opposed to ESTP's dominant function. ESTP prefer actualities to potentialities, what is real to what is possible. When it comes to planning for different scenarios, many ESTP can hardly see the point, preferring to cross those bridges when they come. "Why waste any time worrying about what will happen when we have this present moment to contend with?" an ESTP might ask. Engaged in the here and now, and managing the world in a literal fashion, ESTP have little patience for Ne's abstractions; and when it comes to theories, ESTP only find them suitable if they produce tangible and unfailing results.

ESTP's inner psychology consists most strongly of Ti and, to a lesser degree, Ni. Si and Fi operate outside conscious awareness. With Ti as the top introverted function and the primary method by which they structure information, ESTP can be quite logical and analytical, though in a deeply material way. ESTP instinctively pick up on the basic mechanics of reality and can explain their findings, primarily by means of demonstration; with the right training, ESTP can register the subtlest flavors and textures in a dish and recreate it from scratch. To the extent that this type engages in theoretical pursuits, Ti is the primary vehicle through which that exploration takes place, as it allows ESTP to define terms, check for consistency, verify logical validity, categorize according to like traits and sort matters into true or false. Because ESTP's primary mode of judgment is introverted, they typically do not challenge others' thinking directly; instead ESTP tend to offer concrete facts or ask leading questions. Ti also helps this type navigate the social game competently, as ESTP notice the hidden rules and assumptions that govern the game—generally sporting the right attire for the right event, displaying the right body language and saying the proper things at the proper times. Because Ti is ascendant over Fe in this type, occasional social clumsiness is noted. However, it is typically done with a sincerity that makes ESTP's mistakes easy to forgive.

ESTP get a vague, but powerful sense of the big picture from their inferior Ni. Wrapping its user in an all-encompassing sense of meaning and purpose, Ni gives ESTP a sense of their place in the world and drives them to concrete displays of individuality through this type's dominant function. ESTP rarely receive any of the powerful mental images and pictures that enchant types with Ni further up in their psychic hierarchy and, to the extent ESTP do, the images' importance is habitually minimized. Fortunately, mature ESTP do not engage in such behavior, though the familiar preference for concrete exploration is still noted. Though it tends to function as an archaic and impulsive instinct in this type, Ni is still of the utmost importance to ESTP's psychological health. Ni not only looks beneath the surface of objective phenomena to discover what lies hidden, it also peers behind one's individual psychic curtain, ascertaining the contents and direction of the psyche in the form of archetypes. It is these archetypes, which form the outlines of psychological existence, that direct fates and constitute the patterns of behavior that have been repeated sense time immemorial and will be continued as long as humanity exists—only the outer form, or the garment, of the patterns changes, never the contents. Jung said that Si views sensory experience like one who has existed a million years and had every conceivable experience. Ni, similarly, views the psychic landscape quite as a million-year-old person, easily detecting the direction of any given situation, where it came from and where it is going.[33] Those who integrate the insights that Ni allows to bubble up from the surface are, therefore, at an enormous advantage not only in terms of mental health, but also in terms of their ability to navigate the outer world in a meaningful way.

With Si operating quite unconsciously, ESTP have little regard for history and traditions, and that is all the more the case when tradition seems to prevent needed action. It is not that this type lacks understanding of history, and ESTP are not at all above manipulating traditional viewpoints to meet their agenda. It is just that Si seems to be an artificial limit and, when constricted in such a way, it is almost inevitable that ESTP will seek to push change through like a bulldozer. With Se's desire to focus exclusively on the outside world, Si's preference for comfort over excitement bores ESTP to no end. However, ESTP are quite concerned with maintaining their physical equilibrium because their health is essential to their ability to enjoy life to the fullest. Fi, on the other hand, is far more of an annoyance to ESTP. To this type, feelings belong to the group. ESTP want people to share uplifting feelings or, otherwise, feelings that serve to unite the group around a common theme. With such a viewpoint, it should hardly be shocking that ESTP are deeply out of touch with their personal feelings, showing a similar ignorance of their personal motivations and values as their shadow type, ISTJ, display of collective values and emotional displays. This type, therefore, is prone to a high degree of moral flexibility, heeding only the most fundamental parts of personal ethics with any consistency.

When ESTP's inner and outer psychologies are combined, one finds natural salesmen and politicians. Because of Se, ESTP are incredibly observant, and no type is better in tune with physical reality than ESTP. They deal with the world just as it is, so ESTP notice people's problems and want to come up with tangible solutions to solve them. Because they are so aware of the world around them and the tools at their disposal, ESTP are strong tacticians—their significant expediency only limited by their integrity. Ti allows this type to build an internal framework that explains the rules of the system and helps ESTP explain what they can realistically do to improve the situation. Though, as an introverted function, Ti's rules are necessarily subjective and personalized, Ti helps ESTP define problems clearly and in terms that are logically consistent. Fe puts ESTP firmly in touch with the community and its values; it drives ESTP not only to participate in their communities, but also to work towards improving them. As the primary way of expressing their judgments to the outer world, ESTP's Fe gets a lot of exercise. Ni gives ESTP their famous gut instinct, that ability to land on their feet no matter how daring their jump. More importantly, Ni gives this type a sense of their place in the world, that vague but powerful feeling that ESTP are not some lonely bags of skin, but part of some larger, yet undefinable whole that works to make the world a better place.

ESTP's perceptions are highly polarized toward dominant Se and, thus, away from their inferior Ni. This polarization is not a character flaw, merely the defining characteristic of Se-dominant types. Because of this polarization, ESTP are highly observant of physical reality and much less attentive to their inner life. This type tends to believe that action only counts if it is concrete, feeling that life's mysteries are best explored by living, not by mere contemplation. ESTP have little patience for abstract theories and, to the extent they will tolerate theories at all, their utility must be clear. ESTP like to keep their options open. ESTP know the general direction they want to go in, but they are not interested in planning every pit stop and bathroom break. Just as ESTP sometimes look at Ni-dominant types as too disconnected from the stream of life, Ni-dominant types occasionally look on ESTP as short-sighted, too often giving insufficient consideration to how part interacts with whole. ISTP, who use Ni in the tertiary position, sometimes feel that ESTP are a bit too inclined to action without fully understanding context and goals because action is not always balanced with adequate reflection. ESTP can sometimes come to errant conclusions about meaning because of an unfounded trust in their intuition, which is undifferentiated. ESTP trust the obvious meaning and clear, explicitly stated data, so much of Ni's mental images and symbolism are ignored in favor of what ESTP can see, smell, touch, taste or hear.

ESTP show far less polarization between their auxiliary Ti and tertiary Fe. Because Se is the dominant player in this type's psyche, Ti is not at all free to rob its counterpart, Fe, of the libido it needs to reach awareness. With Ti and Fe operating right next door to each other, ESTP are quite at home with systems of logic. However, Ti builds models based on conclusions reached deductively and, because of Se, ESTP's logical frameworks favor concrete data and experience over theoretical speculation. Not only does Ti give this type facility with logic in an academic sense, Ti also makes ESTP aware of the rules that underpin effective interactions, communications and relationships. Instead of directing the outer world by extraverting their thought as their ISTJ shadow types would, ESTP appeal to the group's values. This type tends to favor cordial, easy-going relationships, but, because Se calls it like it is and Ti seeks truth, ESTP can be blunt and off-putting. However, with Fe operating somewhat consciously, mature ESTP are not at all inclined to hold grudges, and at the right times, ESTP are more than willing to reestablish a broken line of communication, especially if doing so will prove mutually beneficial.

ENFJ

FE	NI
SE	TI
FI	NE
SI	TE

ENFJ are primarily oriented toward the outer world by Fe and, to a lesser extent, Se. Te and Ne operate unconsciously.

With Fe as ENFJ's dominant function, every other function is subject to its rule.

Fe establishes, applies and regulates group values, whether the group be a family, business, community or society at large. Fe governs the laws of effective human interaction as Te governs the laws of effective systems. Never placing the rules above the people to whom they apply, Fe, nonetheless, seeks to impose its will on the environment as much as Te. Unlike Te, however, Fe prefers carrots to sticks. ENFJ are not to be outdone socially; they regularly sport the proper attire, go the extra mile for their peers and build relationships wherever they go. ENFJ expect others to display the proper feelings for the given context; and while ENFJ prefer to lead by making others smile, it is best not to try their patience too much in this regard, for ENFJ can be quite harsh in their delivery when their lines are crossed. Of course, being the social adepts that ENFJ are, such criticism will be delivered at the right time, even if the appropriate time is in the heat of the moment. ENFJ's famous kindness should not obscure their tendency to keep track of all the favors they have doled out; and should those who have received help from ENFJ fail to return the favor when called upon, ENFJ will give them quite a different response to future requests for help.

ENFJ would not be the social experts they are without a way not only to judge and order the outer world, but also perceive it. Hence, ENFJ combine their well-developed Fe with tertiary Se. While ESFJ, who also use Fe in the dominant position, are eminently practical owing to their use of auxiliary Si, ENFJ are much more imaginative. When it comes to expressing collective values in concrete terms, however, ENFJ are not to be outdone. ESFJ, on the other hand, are far less likely to make concrete expression of their values a motivating factor, instead seeking to express their values via ideas and traditional possibilities.

This discrepancy between ENFJ and ESFJ's extraverted style is largely due to their differing tertiary functions, with the ESFJ consciously utilizing Ne, not Se. Both Ne and Se are exploratory, but unlike Ne, Se is not satisfied with exploration of the ideational space, but instead seeks to explore physical reality concretely, always looking for novelty, noting any changes in the immediate environment and enjoying the strongest possible sensory impulses. Thus, ENFJ are not pleased by merely thinking about values or considering values from an intellectual standpoint, instead viewing values as worthless if concrete evidence of those values cannot be observed. "Everyone says the right thing about wage inequality but, somehow, women still earn only $.76 for every dollar men make." "Bob says that he values our relationship, but whenever I would like to spend some quality time together, he is nowhere to be found." More than any other type, ENFJ are prepared to identify and rectify such discrepancies because the combination of Fe and Se seeks to shape the tangible world with the same intensity seen in more famously authoritative types such as ENTJ.

ENFJ are more than able to identify and exploit objective possibilities and potentialities (Ne), readily ascertaining some sense of collective meaning from their unique experience of the world. However, since ENFJ prefer Se to Ne when dealing with the outer world, ENFJ are far more concerned with objective realities, not potentialities. ENFJ are, therefore, not likely to use Ne except to criticize themselves or others. At such times, it is quite easy for ENFJ to point out a whole host of reasons to explain why they have socially marginalized someone, or to whip out a comprehensive list of failures to meet common-sense group values or even to demonstrate that there are many options for improving upon the way collective ideals manifest in daily life. Ne gets used in this way primarily when ENFJ are stressed about or unhappy with real-world results (Se). Te, on the other hand, is a far more challenging matter for ENFJ since they prefer to structure the world of people, not impersonal systems. ENFJ are, consequently, deeply skeptical of Te since it seems to ignore the human factor, at least from a Fe perspective; and though Te-types would argue that giving too much weight to a single person's problems with the system often serves to undermine the system's efficacy for everyone else, ENFJ are left cold because they believe that systems should work for everyone, even those with unique or difficult circumstances.

ENFJ's inner psychology consists most strongly of Ni and, to a lesser degree, Ti, while Fi and Si operate unconsciously. With Ni as the top introverted function and the lens through which they prefer to perceive the world, ENFJ are quite good at getting a grasp of the big picture and, because Ni's most inimitable asset is its ability to sense what lies below phenomenal existence, ENFJ easily pick up on clues about others that would elude types that have Ni further down in their psychic economy. ENFJ, therefore, just know things about people, and receive in the form of mental images and hunches key information regarding other's psychic makeup or constitution. In this regard, all strong Ni-types are alike. However, ENFJ are the most likely to use their insights into others to control the outer world because Fe drives them to people-centric action; and it is because of Fe's combination with auxiliary Ni that ENFJ are regarded as master manipulators—only for good, of course. The drive to action is a key distinguishing feature between ENFJ and their close psychological relative, INFJ.

Though quite skilled socially, INFJ are far more comfortable observing and waiting to push buttons at the most opportune time. On the other hand, ENFJ cannot help but act— immediately applying their insights into others in a concrete way.

ENFJ are socially adept because they have a deep, but undifferentiated, sense of the logic (Ti) that undergirds effective social communication. Because Fe seeks to apply the right values at the right times, it can be prone to a degree of moral flexibility—a key distinguishing trait between Fe and its shadow, Fi. Strong Fe-types work to find common ground, even when the ground is uncomfortable for one side or another. It is just that flexibility, however, that makes Fe-types so effective in the social world. Naturally, this skill demands a logical framework. Different behavior is needed at work than at a party. One dresses differently for dinner at a five-star restaurant than one does for a night at a sports bar. Of course, such categorization is characteristic of Ti. It is not that ENFJ sit around and spend their time defining terms, deducing logical rules and building logical frameworks, though with the proper education, ENFJ are more than capable of doing so—that kind of behavior would be much more common in strong Ti-types. It is just that ENFJ instinctively know the basic rules of the game, appealing to what unites people, even when that demands uniting against others. While not as analytical as INFJ, ENFJ nonetheless have a vague sense of their basic logical assumptions. A characteristic difference between ENFJ and their shadow type, INFP, is that INFP are likely to give credence to facts and expert opinion whereas ENFJ will give weight to their own logical deductions. Because ENFJ's deductions are somewhat vague, ENFJ's conclusions are sometimes a hit-or-miss affair, as any ENFJ has experienced when shunned for coming to the wrong conclusion about others simply because of inadequate consideration of their own reasoning—an error that is in no way limited to this type.

With Fi operating almost completely unconsciously, ENFJ have a much harder time ascertaining their own feelings, values and emotions than they do others'. ENFJ do spend a lot of time working through their feelings alone, but this tends to be more of a logical analysis than a direct confrontation with their core feelings. As a result, ENFJ will often rely on talking through their feelings just to get a sense of what is going on, not necessarily needing another's input—though that might be welcome at the right time. It is simply that by extraverting their own emotions and values, ENFJ can rely on their key strength, Fe. In this way, ENFJ do not deal with their feelings in an internal or reflective way; that would be characteristic of INFP and ISFP. The ENFJ's way of dealing with Fi is, nevertheless, effective enough. Si, on the other hand, is much more of an annoyance to ENFJ. With its deeply traditional approach to life, Si is little more than an appendage to ENFJ's psychology. While mature ENFJ are in tune with their environment, staying in touch with their bodies is much more of a challenge—with ENFJ only paying attention to their bodies when they are in a state of discomfort; and because of their struggles with Si, ENFJ need constant reaffirmation as to how their emotional gestures will be received. Thus, tasks that would be second-nature for ESFJ, like planning an event, are more of a challenge for ENFJ.

When ENFJ's inner and outer personalities are considered in tandem, one finds society's best warrior for a world that reflects the values held by those who inhabit it. ENFJ are the type most likely to make real sacrifices to benefit their communities and organizations—not ideological sacrifices, but concrete ones. ENFJ cannot, not make change, and they tend to feel rather constricted when they occupy roles, jobs or positions in which their capacity to help, develop or improve life for other people is limited. Fe drives ENFJ not only to tune into communal values, but also to shape, re-define and apply those values to the outer world—and ENFJ easily use collectively held values as the vehicle by which their agenda is advanced. Ni allows ENFJ to look past the obvious to find the patterns, meaning and unconscious contents that underlie everyone's experience of the world. Ni also allows ENFJ to sense one's psychic makeup, seeing the person as they are without any labels or titles, and discarding any superfluous elements. With tertiary Se readily available to well-developed members of this type, ENFJ work to apply their psychological insights in a concrete manner, never satisfied with mere contemplation, but always driven to action by a fierce need for closure. Ti not only provides the terms, definitions and classifications essential to Fe's operations, but also helps ENFJ to refine their value judgments to accord with their foundational, yet subjective, logical principles.

ENFJ's judgments are highly polarized toward their feelings and, consequently, away from their thinking function. This polarization is the defining characteristic of any Fe-dominant type. As a result, ENFJ are attuned to the slightest hint of collective valuation, and it is with the values of their families, jobs and communities that ENFJ seek to align. ENFJ are most at home when they are driving toward completion. This type is, therefore, happiest when allowed the space to characterize, define and develop the values that tie groups together. Ti is the function best able to define terms in a logically consistent manner, and it places truth and correctness far above any person, place or thing. Unfortunately, Ti is something of a weak spot for ENFJ since Fe, is free to steal much of the libido to which its counterpart is entitled. It appears that Fe is able to function in such a differentiated manner because Ti is locked in a state of arrested development. Regrettably for ENFJ, the social game (Fe) can never be separated from the logic that underlies it. One can understand this principle by attempting to imagine one's favorite sport being played without the rules and regulations that make fair play possible—even to imagine such a scene borders on absurd. As is common in any type, the intense polarization between their dominant and inferior functions can really backfire when ENFJ fail to account for both sides of the judging process. For example, most ENFJ would admit that they have errantly and publicly ostracized another because ENFJ were so quick to apply their judgment that they overlooked key factors that would have changed their feelings had the ENFJ considered the factors.

With Ni and Se in closer proximity, ENFJ show far less polarity between those functions. Because Fe is the dominant player in this type's psyche, Ni is not at all free to rob its counterpart, Se, of the libido necessary to reach consciousness. ENFJ shift seamlessly from looking beyond the obvious to acting based on their insight. As a result, ENFJ are not only more likely than INFJ to assert their values and speak on behalf of the group's feelings, but also more likely to act on their psychological insights. Se understands the world in a concrete way and is much more satisfied than Ni to limit its perception to the present situation and its challenges. While Se is by no means ENFJ's strong suit, they still are not as susceptible to the perceptual errors that occasionally trip up INFJ because ENFJ are more likely to make sure that their intuitive insights match the concrete data. On the other hand, INFJ sometimes let their imaginations run wild. The tradeoff, of course, is ENFJ's intuitive insights seldom show the depth or the power of INFJ's, who often see the very heart of the matter with the scantest effort.

Psychology of Si-Ne, Fi-Te Types

ISTJ

SI	TE
FI	NE
SE	TI
FE	NI

ISTJ are primarily oriented to their inner worlds, which are consciously influenced by Si and, to a lesser extent, Fi. Ti and Ni operate unconsciously.

Because Si is the dominant function, all ISTJ's other functions are necessarily subordinate to its demands.

Si lends awareness of the internal aspects of sensory experience. It records one's history in sharp detail and has a curious way of perpetuating tradition. Most in its element when following routine, Si hates risks and is thrown into a state of discomfort at the slightest sign of change, especially when change applies to abstractions like ideas and theories. ISTJ are, therefore, unassuming and practical people with a deep passion for predictability. Consideration of their shadow type, ESTP, can help illuminate some of ISTJ's inner workings. With Se as their dominant function, ESTP are intensely aware of their environment, seeking sensory stimulus like a great white shark seeks chum, never afraid of the unexpected and always prepared for an enjoyable time. With the same fervor that ESTP pursue intensity of objective sensory experience, ISTJ search for personal comfort and familiarity. Where ESTP love to focus on perceiving the world exactly as it is, ISTJ are profoundly aware of how the world appears to them and, from such a tendency, ISTJ derive an enormous advantage. As much as Se-types might hate to admit it, the subjective side of sensory perception can never be removed, only stifled. Instead of remaining unconscious of this necessary aspect of human psychology, ISTJ give Si their full attention.

As any person with enough life experience knows, there are many traditions and routines, many interpretations of history, many risks to minimize. Logic, whether deductive or empirical, is powerless to resolve conflicting values. ISTJ, therefore, need a reliable way to decide what matters most when these preferences come into conflict and members of this type reach resolution by getting in touch with their feelings about their routines, habits and traditions.

ISTJ utilize Fi as their tertiary function and it is a part of their psychological makeup that is often overlooked. Fi makes one aware of one's personal values, ethics and emotions. Unwilling to act in any manner contrary to their core beliefs, types who consciously use Fi are deeply principled in public and private, and when pushed too far, these types can be rather brutal in their efforts to ensure that their principles are protected. When Fi occupies the tertiary position, it can be childlike in its judgments. That means ISTJ have not only a child's charming sincerity and earnestness, but also the tendency to judge values in black and white. Because Fi is so closely linked with Si in this type, mature ISTJ often become aware of emotional distress through a disturbance in their bodies; unwelcome news in the morning is followed by a debilitating stomach ache; anxiety about a date accompanied by sweaty palms; an employee's disrespectful tirade trailed by high blood pressure. While they have a similar tendency, ESTJ's ability to read the links between their physical equilibrium and emotional state is diminished in comparison to ISTJ's, who are more skilled with both Si and Fi than their ESTJ cousins. With their refined tastes, ISTJ like to enjoy the finer things in life, valuing the comfort of luxury and the joy of an occasional indulgence as fair reward for their hard work and unfailing dedication to their families, organizations and communities. Like INTJ, ISTJ are far more sensitive than their stoic appearance might indicate. Fi is conscious enough for ISTJ to have at least a rudimentary sense of their feelings and beliefs, but ISTJ's skill with Fi is not always strong enough to work through difficult emotions. Emotional wounds, therefore, cut deep for this type. However, ISTJ are not driven by a desire to be liked, instead believing that it "is much safer to be feared than loved, when, of the two, either must be dispensed with."[34]

ISTJ prefer to extravert their thinking, using it to structure the world around them. Eminently practical and characteristically steady, ISTJ see little need for a deductive approach to logic. "The facts are the facts, no reason to complicate matters with fancy jargon," an ISTJ might say. Though they tend to show some facility at using Ti because it has much in common with Te, ISTJ generally reserve Ti's use for criticism of themselves or others. Ti appears most often when a deeply held Fi value has been trampled. When Ti does show up in ISTJ, they can get very serious about defining terms and ascertaining logical validity, using Ti as a ferocious instrument of conflict, despite ISTJ's normally calm nature. Ni, on the other hand, ISTJ tend to find more taxing since it is the function most opposed to ISTJ's dominant Si. Both functions keep an eye toward the inner world, but Si is concerned largely with physical processes, while Ni focuses on psychic processes. ISTJ have little interest in what it views as Ni's esoteric and unfounded predictions about the future, and ISTJ tend to believe most in what they have experienced themselves. It seems that the possibility that the psyche is a world onto itself—and a world worth exploring—is not fully appreciated by this type, in much the same way that Ni-dominant types seem to have little regard for the traditions and routines that bring ISTJ so much stability and comfort.

ISTJ's extraverted psychology is the result of auxiliary Te's interaction with inferior Ne. Se and Fe operate unconsciously. With Te as the chief extraverted function and their preferred mode of judgment, ISTJ are serious people, driven by a desire to get measurable results for their efforts and a fierce need to maximize efficiency. Members of this type lay down as many guidelines, policies and procedures as needed to reach their objectives, and enforce rules with impartiality. Never interested in managing others' values and feelings, ISTJ treat thought as belonging to the community and feelings as belonging to individuals. ISTJ, therefore, direct systems and outcomes, dealing with the people aspect only insofar as the system depends it. Te standardizes methods, codifies terms and regulates procedures to produce consistent, actionable results. Like all Te-types, ISTJ not only value competence, they demand it, and with their tendency to take a deep dive into the details, it is best to ensure that any work an ISTJ might be inspecting meets the agreed upon specifications—ISTJ can be ruthless in their ability to weed out errors, and onlookers can easily be taken aback by the bluntness of ISTJ's delivery. Te packages data in a literal form, and Te-types often have impeccable memories for facts and figures; when combined with Si, which is the memory powerhouse of the cognitive functions, Te gives ISTJ the best memories of all the types.

Much of ISTJ's Te usage is aimed at managing possibilities spotted by Ne and, because it is this type's inferior function, Ne tends to spot possibilities of the negative variety. "A high-risk, high-reward approach to investment is unacceptable. Put my money in a diversified portfolio meant to deliver steady, long-term growth," an ISTJ might say. ISTJ are less likely to ask what-if questions and explore open-ended scenarios than remember what has been and associate the present with cherished memories. Preparing for the future with an eye toward those strategies whose effectiveness is well established and arguing that if a possibility is truly plausible, there ought to be historical precedent for that plausibility, mature ISTJ can often explain how a current problem is like one previously encountered and offer realistic solutions based on what has worked in the past. Though ISTJ's solutions rarely show the creative flair of a strong Ne-type's, ISTJ's pragmatism and reliability still win this type plaudits from those who know them best. ISTJ rarely demonstrate the verbal fluency of ENTP or ENFP, but Ne gives many ISTJ a healthy dose of wittiness, even though the function is undifferentiated in this type.

ISTJ are not as in tune with the outside world and the latest trends as they are with their bodies and familiar customs, and because ISTJ are so focused on the details of their subjective sensory experience, many of the details of the outside world elude this type. ISTJ can walk by someone who is saying their name and completely miss it. That is not to say that ISTJ use Se incompetently or completely lack awareness of physical reality. There is no inner sensory experience (Si) without outer objects (Se) to stimulate it, and since ISTJ are Si adepts, they naturally accumulate a degree of competence with Se — almost like a side effect. Fe, on the other hand, is more difficult for ISTJ, and no other function frustrates them more. Because ISTJ prefer to use Te to run their outer lives, they tend to feel phony when making Fe displays, and that is only natural. However, ISTJ often project the same sense of inauthenticity onto others' Fe usage, forgetting that a core goal of Fe's is to facilitate cordial relationships and neglecting to recognize that Fe users are sincere in their efforts at harmonizing.

When ISTJ's inner and outer psychologies are combined, one finds a natural historian. ISTJ are deeply aware of their pasts and traditions. Because Si puts one in touch with one's own experience of the world, ISTJ are conscious of the details that make up their daily lives. ISTJ are most at ease when they can dig into the specifics and uncover clues that are hiding in plain sight; and because of their willingness to work the details patiently, representatives of this type are able to unearth treasures that others have overlooked in haste. ISTJ structure the outer world for ease and efficiency. In forming their judgments, ISTJ simply want the facts and figures. Concerned about fairness and objectivity, ISTJ set forth clear criteria for their judgments before taking measurements, and ISTJ prefer empirical validation as tests of validity to deductive conclusions. Deeply moral, this type sticks to its standards of right and wrong, and ISTJ are generally better than Te-dominant types at deciding what is most important to them, what motivates them, what lines they will never cross. Though ISTJ often help others put the present situation into a historical context, this type has a vague and unconscious expectation that the future will be like the past. To the extent that ISTJ seriously consider the future, it is usually to ward off negative possibilities, securing their forts in preparation for life's storms; for, above all else, ISTJ anticipate what will go wrong.

ISTJ's perceptions are highly polarized toward their dominant Si and, thus, away from their inferior Ne. ISTJ trust their personal experiences and backgrounds as measures of the truth, and this type is skeptical of deductive arguments, value judgments and, worst of all, intuitive speculation, whose insights ISTJ find lacking. ISTJ value physical comfort and stability above all else, so this type makes enormous effort to minimize risk and ensure a future for themselves and families that will be secure from economic swings. With so much of their worldview based in their memories, ISTJ rely on habit and routine to help bring order to the world. Because ISTJ are so observant, there is a greater gap between insight and action, perception and judgment than one encounters in ESTJ, who are often most certain about what they are thinking when they can talk it out. While this might mean that ISTJ's output is somewhat diminished in comparison, it also means that a higher percentage of their work will make the cut since they spend so much time reflecting before acting. As introverts, ISTJ rarely demonstrate the same verbal fluency that ESTJ do, but ISTJ tend to have insightful things to say when they do chime in, usually taking note of the obvious facts that everyone is overlooking.

ISTJ's judgments are far less polarized. Because Si is the dominant player in their psyche, auxiliary Te is not free to use up the libido needed for tertiary Fi to reach consciousness. ISTJ respect authority, title and stature, and believe that problems are best solved when everyone relies on authority figures to make the big decisions; those decisions may not be perfect, but it is better than the chaos that might otherwise ensue. Like INTJ, ISTJ make capable leaders, but they are not at all grasping to control others; this type only wants to ensure that rules, procedures and policies are followed. Though ISTJ can certainly be blunt, just like any strong Te-type, they are generally much more temperate than their ESTJ peers, not because they are emotionally weak, but because their superior emotional intelligence makes them consider the extent to which a wounded warrior will be able contribute to the mission. Despite their often cold and unfeeling appearance, ISTJ are quite sensitive, not to impersonal criticism, but to attacks on their integrity or character. ISTJ can also be distinguished from ESTJ by the latter's tendency to treat each part of their projects — each policy, every infraction — with equal importance. This is a result of Fi's role as ESTJ's inferior function. ISTJ, however, have a clearer sense of what matters most to their goals, and they tend to moderate or increase their efforts based on those evaluations.

INFP

FI	NE
SI	TE
FE	NI
SE	TI

INFP are primarily oriented toward their inner worlds, which are consciously influenced by Fi and, to a lesser extent, Si. Ni and Ti are used unconsciously.

Because Fi is the dominant function, all INFP's other functions play second fiddle to Fi's demands.

Fi puts one in touch with the very core of one's beliefs, motivations, root assumptions, hopes and fears. When Fi is developed to its very highest levels, it picks up on the finest shades of ethical and moral nuance, making it nearly impossible for INFP to act in any way contrary to self. Despite its nuance, Fi seems inflexible when compared to its shadow function, Fe. Because Fi, when left to its own devices, seeks to establish and uphold its values no matter the context, it can sometimes seem to ignore social niceties and fronts in a way that would be unconscionable to a strong Fe-type. "Tonight, my best friend is celebrating her birthday with a party, but I'm too tired to go out." "I know that it is making my colleagues a bit uncomfortable, but I just can't talk to John again after he dismissed my contributions to the team." INFP, far more than Fe-types, follow their feelings no matter where those feelings might lead, even into the deepest darkest tunnels, or the dreaded dark night of the soul. However, INFP are far more willing to tolerate suffering of a psychic nature than physical, which is just the opposite tendency observed in ISFP. This INFP tendency is the result of INFP's auxiliary Ne, which focuses on objective possibilities, not the physical world.

Of all the types with dominant or auxiliary Fi, INFP are the most adamant about remaining true to their values. This is because INFP combine their Fi with tertiary Si, which not only seeks to help INFP maintain some sense of physical equilibrium, but also attaches a significant part of INFP's sense of self to their experiences and valued traditions. It is from this sense of tradition that INFP moralizing emerges.

Si highly values familiarity, stability and routine, and though most INFP descriptions fail to take note of Si's role in this type's psyche, one cannot truly understand INFP's mind without reckoning with this type's tertiary function. Si honors hierarchy, routine, habit and tradition, and so do INFP, if the traditions in question do not trample on INFP's sense of right and wrong; e.g., an INFP who has concluded that racism is a great evil will not tolerate it, no matter how strong the tradition might be. Perhaps Si's most important role for INFP is that of the canary in the coal mine. With Fi and Si so closely linked, mature INFP have surely come to recognize that their emotional states are reflected in how their bodies feel. Feelings of happiness and joy are accompanied by elevated levels of energy and a sense of physical wellbeing. On the other hand, headaches, sweaty palms or tense muscles often accompany negative emotions. In this way, mature INFP become aware of their feelings not only by directly observing their Fi in action, but by seeing how Si reacts — even identifying the cause of an emotion by tracing the corresponding physical state back to its source. In theory, ENFP also have this ability, but because Si occupies the inferior slot, ENFP are not as aware of the link between their internal feelings and sensations.

INFP prefer to use their intuition in an objective fashion and, therefore, their primary use of Ni's subjective approach is to criticize themselves and others. This ability to use Ni, even in this constricted manner, indicates that INFP's conscious use of Ne naturally results in some degree of skill at Ni usage. Thus, INFP are not only able to string together possibilities and probabilities, but also able to get some sense of the psychic substrate that unites all those possibilities and probabilities. INFP prefer Si to Ni, so one will only detect Ni coming into relief if there is an issue that Si is unable to mediate according to its traditional approach. When their values have been crossed, INFP can get quite personal, picking up on character flaws thought to be hidden well out of sight, and INFP easily elucidate, even darkly, what is really going on — promptly going for the jugular in effort to inflict a wound of similar depth on others to what they, themselves, have experienced. Ti, on the other hand, challenges INFP far more because Ti's cold calculations are anathema to Fi's desire to do what feels right. Thus, while INFP always know exactly what they are feeling, they do not tend to show strong awareness of the subjective logic and assumptions that affect their worldview and, therefore, their deepest values.

INFP's extraverted psychology is the result of auxiliary Ne's interaction with inferior Te. Unconscious use of Fe and Se also plays a role. With Ne as the lead extraverted function, INFP are enamored by possibilities, particularly possibilities that bring about positive emotions. Outwardly, INFP have little desire to deal with the physical world as it is, often finding fault with the people and systems that have led to the current state of affairs;

yet INFP are aspirational. "When I first met little Johnny, he was really struggling with his reading assignments, and though he still has a long way to go, my private tutoring of him is already showing real results. I think he could be caught up with the rest of his classmates in a month." The desire to find and express authentic happiness means that INFP share much in common with ISFP. Because ISFP use Se, however, their joy seeking tends to be concrete and practical. On the other hand, INFP tend to see the outer world as much more abstract and, thus, INFP tend to come across as lighter, fluffier and far less grounded than ISFP. One should not be fooled by appearances, however. The same practicality that ISFP show the world exists internally for INFP, while INFP's open-minded, philosophical approach to the outer world exists in ISFP's introverted psychology.

It would be a cruel punishment to hold values as strongly as INFP do but have no way to uphold those values or bring them a tangible reality. That's why Te is so critical to INFP. Te allows one to impose order on the outer world in the form of rules, regulations, laws and policies; and Te does that not just for the sake of organizing the outer world, but also to provide sufficient space and boundaries for each individual to hold and honor his unique beliefs and ethics—within reason, of course. Fe plays a similar role by providing a framework for positive and productive interactions that allows people to reason as they see fit, not according to some standard *out there* in the world. INFP can straddle that line with ease because, on one hand, they care about objective rules and regulations only insofar as rules and regulations help protect individuals and, on the other hand, INFP's deep knowledge of their own values makes it quite natural to respect those who have different beliefs. No function is as ready to tell it like it is as Te and, though INFP's Te shows almost no differentiation, INFP are no exception to the rule. INFP are willing to bite their tongues for quite a while, but when a cherished value has been crossed, INFP can become quite harsh in calling attention to it.

With Fe as the shadow of INFP's dominant Fi, INFP thoroughly understand the rules of the social game. They can be quite good at making others feel at ease and valued. However, that skill should not be assumed to mean INFP regard understanding and manipulating social dynamics as central to their way of operating in the world. When their role in the group does not contradict their personal feelings, INFP are quite happy to play along. The moment there is a discrepancy between the group's values and INFP's, however, expect INFP to use their Te to either point out the discrepancy and come up with steps to fix it, or conclude that they would sooner run for the hills than act, think or feel in any way contrary to what they truly believe. If those two options are unavailable, however, INFP will fall into the dominant-tertiary loop in which Fi constantly points out this type's negative valuation of the situation, but Si does nothing more than to point out that this is the way things have always been and, thus, confers the feeling that change is impossible. With that said, Se is INFP's sore spot, and because of it, INFP have gained an unfair reputation for being all talk, no action. On one hand, INFP admire Se-types' willingness to get their hands dirty and make concrete changes to the world, though INFP often consider such change to be cosmetic. On the other hand, INFP's preference for the comparatively conservative Si causes them to cling to what is most familiar and comfortable; physical novelty, then, is something INFP typically loathe.

When INFP's inner and outer psychologies are put together, one finds the humanitarian. Fi gives INFP a near-singular insight into their own values, and because INFP also use Ne, those values tend to relate to ideas, beliefs and possibilities. Si helps to confine those possibilities to the ones that accord with tradition and practical experience, and Te steps in to provide the factual support and planning needed to apply personal value judgments to the outer world. This unique setup means INFP not only provide the guidance and support needed to help others grow, but also that INFP live and let live — never seeking to tell others how to feel and showing great deference to individual values as long as the rules and system are shown the proper respect. In this way, INFP differ sharply from strong Fe-types, who apply their value judgments directly to the outer world and insist that people display the proper emotions for the situation and etiquette for their social role. Fi-types, however, must either hint at their value judgments using Ne or, otherwise, impose the judgment using inferior thought. With such a rich emotional life, no one knows life's greatest joys better than INFP but, because opposites always unite, it is also the case that no one knows life's sorrows better either. Despite their gracious style, no type is better equipped to deal with an emotional maelstrom than INFP though, like all people, it is not what they would prefer. Desire, no matter how well intentioned, does not mean that one gets to acquire — a lesson that is in no way unique to INFP, but one that they are forced to confront constantly because their desires are so palpable. Indeed, this kind of suffering is built into the psychic mechanism and, as a result, INFP are incredibly resilient people. It also means that INFP are prepared to lay down the law when necessary, never viewing personal feelings as sufficient reason to disregard the rules.

INFP show a good deal of polarization toward their feelings and, therefore, away from their thinking, and though the road to individuation means bringing greater balance between the dominant and inferior functions, this polarization is nonetheless a defining characteristic of INFP. This polarization is the natural consequence of Fi taking for itself much of the libido to which Te is entitled. INFP's brand of dominant-inferior polarization means they find the slightest shades of nuance in matters of right or wrong, good or bad, like or dislike. However, the road between those realizations and action is often a long one—a journey INFP are not too willing to hazard without a compelling emotion or value providing the fuel and, as soon as the fuel is spent, INFP struggle to continue. While this tendency is sometimes used to give INFP a good-natured ribbing, it is a tendency that is of the utmost significance to the rest of the world. When one is thrown into the furnace of life, one often finds that it is nearly impossible to maintain perfect harmony between belief and action, ideal and result, things wished for and things that must be accepted. By keeping so much space between value and action, INFP ensure that their values maintain a high degree of purity, rarely compromised by expedience or so-called necessity. Thus, while this polarization is not something to be cherished, there is nothing wrong with acknowledging the benefits that such a point of view confers on humanity.

There is far less polarization between INFP's intuition and sensation, which is the natural consequence of auxiliary intuition leaving sufficient libido free for tertiary sensation to emerge into consciousness. INFP, thus, shift between tradition and novelty, body and mind with relative ease. Though INFP are traditional, comfort-loving people in their private lives, they like to be at the cutting edge of society in their public lives — cutting edge meaning the place where they can make the most impact on people's lives with the least effort. They differ from ISFP in this regard because, unlike ISFP, INFP are not interested in fighting on the battlefield for their values but, instead, providing needed intellectual guidance — reminding society that the purpose of its rules and laws is to protect individuals, not drown individuals in a sea of anonymity. No matter how innovative their sense of the possibilities might be, INFP are always sure to find plenty of support for their position, not only because of their often-overwhelming sincerity, but also because the values INFP work to uphold are humanity's timeless moral and ethical understandings.

ESTJ

TE	SI
NE	FI
TI	SE
NI	FE

ESTJ are primarily oriented to the outer world by Te and, to a lesser degree, Ne. Fe and Se operate unconsciously.

With Te as ESTJ's dominant function, every other function is subordinate to its demands.

Te orders the outside world in an impersonal fashion. It provides the rules, policies, procedures and laws that govern effective organizations, communities and societies. Never vague or lacking for factual support, Te structures the outer world for efficiency, and Te-types are by far the most direct and aggressive in their efforts to impose order. Te-types do not behave this way because they lack consideration for others, but because they recognize how much people suffer when the rules of the game are not clearly defined and standardized — or worse, when the rules are not enforced. Where Fe seeks to structure the world of people by establishing rapport and sharing values, Te seeks to build and improve the systems in which people operate. ESTJ, thus, are disciplined people, dealing with the world in a practical way and measuring themselves and others according to a clear set of standards. In consideration of these traits, one can hardly wonder why ESTJ are so prone to leadership and at home in the upper ranks of management. Organized and decisive, one can always expect ESTJ to come prepared with the facts and this type will debate to the end, throwing out a multitude of data and information that can overwhelm those who are not prepared. ESTJ often display a good amount of verbal fluidity and present themselves well in front of others. When mature, representatives of this type easily spot the links between the structure of a system and the consequences that structure implies.

ESTJ can be disposed to a degree of stagnation, partially due to Te's apparent rigidity. Fortunately, tertiary Ne not only provides the primary content of ESTJ's view of the outer world, but also helps ESTJ keep their options open and foresee logical outcomes.

Ne perceives the potentials inherent in sensory data, moving from narrow consideration of that data to wider and wider circles of possibilities, building a spider web of associations. With its propensity for asking what-if questions, Ne can be something of a destabilizing force, but any such tendencies are due to Ne's attempts to bring any nascent possibilities to the surface. Because Te is so practical and literal, it can have a tough time foreseeing far-ranging empirical results, especially if there is little practical experience with which to work. When Te is paired with a healthy amount of intuition, it can take an expansive view, making plans that anticipate consequences years into the future and incorporating contingencies directly into the system. Given mature ESTJ's combination of empirical thinking with an ability to perceive objective possibilities clearly, it should be no surprise that this type makes for excellent tacticians and planners, especially when ESTJ have practical experience with the terrain to be traversed. ESTJ's verbal fluidity is largely due to Ne, which spots the links between contrasting ideas and expounds upon those links, often in humorous ways. Because the tertiary function is mostly undifferentiated, ESTJ often have a black-and-white view of intuitive matters and view much of the intuitive exploration of strong Ne-types as something of a waste, concluding that excessive exploration is not only anathema to ESTJ's traditional approach to life, but also risky.

Fe can be especially challenging for ESTJ, who already have enough trouble sorting out their personal morals and feelings (Fi). This problem is in no way helped by the fact that Fe is the function most strongly opposed to Te. On one hand, ESTJ do appreciate some help with Fe because, like Te, it structures the outer world. To expect ESTJ to use Fe actively, however, is asking for too much. ESTJ care so deeply about the rules because the rules provide a map for the successful navigation of the outer world and Fe, with its penchant for giving near-total attention to the people in the immediate environment, often seems to undermine systems by setting individuals above the whole group the system was designed for in the first place. In other words, Fe can prove a frustration for Te-types, who see Fe as willing to destabilize an entire system in service of maintaining harmonious interactions between a subset of individuals within the system. Though Se is largely unconscious in ESTJ, they are still quite capable of wielding it on occasion. Members of this type reserve Se's use for criticism, whether the criticism is directed at themselves or others. When Se comes out, ESTJ can get quite bellicose and determined to crush the competition, aggressively challenging what they deem absurd with a torrent of concrete figures and data that cannot be ignored.

ESTJ's inner world is most driven by Si and, to a lesser extent, Fi. Ni and Ti operate unconsciously. Since Si is their top introverted function and preferred mode of perception, ESTJ are in touch with their personal histories and traditions. Si only begins its perceptions with the objects of the outer world; it is what objects unleash within that draws its interest. Not so interested in the world *as it is*, Si is more driven by how the world *appears* to its user. Where Se is driven by the intensity of the outer world, seeking thrills and new experience, Si thrives on familiarity and the comfort that comes along with it. ESTJ easily keep track of details, not only because of outstanding memories, but because this type's consistent habits produce reliable results; and though ESTJ are far more exploratory in their outer psychological makeup than ISTJ, ESTJ are quite cautious and prudent in their daily lives, and regularly defer to the tried-and-true approach over the speculative whenever it is a matter of import.

ESTJ use Fi in the inferior position and, therefore, have a deep, but undifferentiated, urge to make the world just and fair.

That urge compels ESTJ to uphold and defend those systems designed to support such values. This type is already opinionated owing to dominant Te, and ESTJ can hardly rest until they set errors of fact or reasoning right. ESTJ do not do so to be mean or harsh, but because it would not be right to allow someone they value to walk around with errant beliefs. Inferior Fi also makes it hard to convince ESTJ once they have made their minds up on a matter. Fi can be internally dogmatic to begin with, but with it in the inferior slot, ESTJ show no compunction about making their dogmas known to the outer world and using those dogmas as justification for rules and regulations that sometimes do more harm in the form of damaged relationships than good. Moreover, because establishing importance is one of Fi's trademarks, it often appears that this type is willing to go to war over the slightest lapse in judgment or belief. The result being, ESTJ's famous efficiency undermined by assigning equal importance to each part of their projects, micromanaging to control every detail and losing others' support when it really counts — the ESTJ having spent too much time beating up others over trivialities. Despite these typical weaknesses, mature ESTJ are more than willing to be held to the same standards to which they hold others. ESTJ's leadership is cherished not only for its executive presence, which steadies those under this type's direction, but also because inherent in ESTJ's psychological makeup is a desire to meet the same moral obligations in private as expected in public. Over time, mature ESTJ's willingness to meet their highest moral obligations wins this type support from those near and far, and ESTJ, in turn, seek to ensure that those morals are passed down in the form of tradition.

Though ESTJ use Ti unconsciously, they are still able to demonstrate some competence with the function in short bursts. ESTJ can categorize, define terms and form valid logical deductions, but this type is most comfortable when it can do so using real-world premises. The more abstract the logic becomes, the less comfortable ESTJ will be, not because ESTJ are incapable along those lines, but because it is hard for them to get the point of overly theoretical systems of explanation, believing that proof is in the pudding, not in logical deductions. With Ti being limited by its largely unconscious use and Fi shorthanded by its undifferentiated state, ESTJ's endless drive to organize the outer world can best be seen as symptomatic of an inner world that is free flowing and loosely structured because all opposites must balance psychologically. Though ESTJ are inwardly perceptive, ESTJ tend to look on Ni with a deep degree of distrust. Ne taken too far is already a headache but throw in Ni's bizarre ability to see beyond the obvious and one quickly begins to understand the reason for ESTJ's utter distaste of Ni—distaste that is in no way lessened by Ni's tendency to undermine Si's preference for routine and stability. Because Ni is the function most strongly opposed to ESTJ's preferred mode of perception, it seems to overlook key details with a glaring casualness and piece together a picture from the scantest data points. If Ni's apparent glibness is not disaster to the careful, meticulous and methodical ESTJ, what could be? ESTJ occasionally worry about the future, their tertiary Ne a vehicle for spotting all the things that could go wrong. Si, therefore, is used to get a sense of the what has occurred in the past to eliminate every risk possible. Ni, with its innate ability to peer deep into the future, is of little comfort to ESTJ, who sometimes find in the future reasons to fear, where a strong Ni-type would undoubtedly notice a clear road to success.

When ESTJ's outer and inner personalities are combined, one finds the archetypal admiral. ESTJ are nothing if not empirical. They want the numbers, facts, data — their opponent's location. Comfortable making the tough choices, ESTJ are natural leaders and struggle in roles that do not allow them to make use of their managerial talent. This type upholds rules, policies and regulations without the slightest hesitation. ESTJ are undeterred from asserting their opinions and conclusions with firmness, sometimes wounding others without a bit of malicious intent. Moving from Point A to Point B with purpose, mature ESTJ know how to advance their strategic interests without rocking the boat, which is because this type is deeply attuned to tradition. Members of this type believe that in abandoning one's traditions, one abandons oneself. The routines on which ESTJ rely help anchor them in a safe harbor, away from the sometimes-turbulent sea of life. ESTJ can spot many consequences and direct their troops toward the desired outcome and away from the disastrous ones. When mature, ESTJ, are capable strategists, using their intuition to detect adverse possibilities and adjust their tactics. ESTJ follow the timeless and fundamental notions of right and wrong, and while they appreciate outside advice on value judgments, they prefer to make such decisions themselves. ESTJ can be cold and emotionally unavailable, but they will generally stick to their guns on moral issues and conduct business with fairness and integrity.

ESTJ's judgments are highly polarized away from their inferior Fi and, therefore, toward their dominant Te. ESTJ are very good at structuring their outer lives. They accurately measure resources and deploy their assets at the most opportune time. Decisive and objective, ESTJ favor immediate action and assess the results. Not well in tune with their own feelings and emotions, ESTJ are not at all controlling of the emotional atmosphere or how others might feel — if ESTJ even notice, that is. Members of this type are firm about demanding complete compliance from all under their command, and sometimes this can take the form of bullying since ESTJ are not at all likely to realize they have crossed the line until they have had some quiet time for reflection. However, before ESTJ have time to work through their process, it is often too late, the wounds they left, too deep. Mature ESTJ handle respectful criticism well and, in fact, welcome others' input as a way to improve their plans and calculations. It is best to be mindful of one's rank in offering an appraisal, however. Because they are in tune with protocol and custom, ESTJ respect status, title and position; and when presented with arguments of equal power, ESTJ will give credence to the conclusions of the higher-ranking officer. Less mature ESTJ, on the other hand, are easily wounded by impersonal criticism, taking it as an affront to their value as a human being. That flaw notwithstanding, ESTJ count personal integrity in high regard, and they will do what is right even when they dislike the person affected.

There is far less polarization in ESTJ's perceptions than in their judgments. ESTJ's dominant function prevents auxiliary Si from robbing tertiary Ne of its libido. ESTJ are most comfortable when they are in familiar territory, and because ESTJ value comfort and stability more than most else, they stick to what they know. ESTJ would rather keep things the way they have always been, viewing change with caution, no matter how carefully considered the change might be; and while ESTJ do not view the future with the same degree of pessimism as ISTJ, who use inferior Ne, there is little ESTJ hate more than risk. Mature representatives of this type are intellectually curious and display verbal ease and fluency. ESTJ are not terribly reflective, however, so they are most likely to refine their opinions when sharing their thoughts and receiving feedback. Deeply aware of historical trends, ESTJ are never at a loss for how to relate present challenges to past difficulties.

ENFP

NE	FI
TE	SI
NI	FE
TI	SE

ENFP are chiefly oriented to the outer world by means of Ne and, to a lesser degree, tertiary Te. Each type uses every cognitive function, so ENFP also use Se and Fe, though these functions are used unconsciously.

With Ne as the dominant function, every other function is subordinate to Ne's demands.

Ne readily and easily perceives the comings and goings of objective possibilities and potentialities. While it might be tempting to marvel at how something that is a mere possibility can ever be objective, it is necessary to remember what objective means in this context. By objective is meant any sensation, feeling, thought or intuition that is an object of perception. Clearly, some possibilities apply to the subject and can only make sense to the person who perceives them. There are, however, some possibilities that apply to the world outside of oneself, and such possibilities are objective. For example, Jill has been a great customer service manager, but based on her credentials, she could make an even bigger impact as a marketing executive. Unlike INFJ, whose intuitions are subjective, but always pertaining to objective, observable sensory data, ENFP's objective intuition always bears clear relation to a subjective, unique sensory experience. ENFP executives might look at a piece of technology and sense its enormous potential to alter the business climate. Because ENFP are well in tune with objective meaning, they are very good at picking the right words and symbols to express their feelings, goals and ideas, and ENFP are among the best public speakers — motivating others with their often-significant powers of persuasion.

Since Ne is this type's most differentiated function, ENFP are able to use it to hunt down opportunities that would elude less observant types. Making all those possibilities realities, however, requires extraverted judgment, not only to take the necessary steps and actions needed to reach the desired outcome, but to determine if the final product meets the specifications.

With Te as the chief extraverted judging function, ENFP tend to come across as far more organized and disciplined in the outer world than their ENTP cousins. ENTP tend to manage the outer world by effectively using their relationships, connections and sense of group values to manipulate the world to their desired outcome. ENFP, however, tend to impose a systems-based order on the outer world, which is characteristic of Te. "I always brush my teeth from left to right to ensure that I don't miss any." "Last time I saw Thomas, he was quite rude to my new friend, so I demanded an apology, blocked him from all of my social media accounts and told him never to call me again." "I want to reduce the amount I'm spending on gas, so instead of running today's errands randomly, I'll start with the stop farthest from my house and end with the stop nearest home." Mature ENFP make for surprisingly strong strategists because not only do ENFP pick up on objectively possible outcomes, this type's Te is developed enough to drive relentlessly towards effective closure. That is not to say that ENFP are masters of Te, even when mature. Just as ENTP's tertiary Fe tends to make values quite black and white, so too is ENFP's tertiary Te prone to relying on this-or-that formulations to structure the outer world, even when types with more-developed Te would see that there are other roads to the same destination.

ENFP are generally quite aware of the correct social protocols, standards and values at work in the situations this type encounters, and because ENFP expect to see their personal values acknowledged and respected by others, ENFP are willing to help uphold group values (Fe). ENFP, however, are most comfortable when they are true to their own values, not a group's. Thus, ENFP's primary use of Fe is to criticize themselves and others; and when they are hurt, ENFP are not above playing social games meant to make another feel like an outcast. Since ENFP's Fe is largely unconscious and, therefore, unpolished, ENFP often end up looking petty and shallow — unable to conceal their true motivations since those motivations are so close to the surface. These kinds of social games are best left to the types with strong Fe. When ENFP lash out via Fe, it is generally not because of a direct violation of a group value, but because one's actions have undermined objective systems from which ENFP have derived comfort and stability. Se, on the other hand, is a more challenging matter for ENFP. Not at all in touch with the physical world around them, ENFP will tend to struggle with basic matters like remembering where they put their wallets or noticing insignificant movements in the environment.

ENFP's inner world is most driven by Fi and, to a lesser extent, Si. Ni and Ti are used unconsciously. Since Fi is the top introverted function, ENFP are deeply aware of their beliefs, motivations and values. Those who spend the most time around ENFP know that members of this type would rather walk on hot coals than act in any way contrary to themselves. As a result, some selfishness is noted. To focus on that minor shortcoming, however, is to forget that ENFP are truly humanitarians at heart and, because of Fi, ENFP will stop at no lengths to help those who have moved them to compassion. Therefore, ENFP would assert that their apparent selfishness is no selfishness, simply a belief that he can best help others who can best help himself. Fi is especially significant since with so many possibilities under consideration, ENFP need some way to ascertain not only which possibilities are most likely to become reality, but also which ones are worth pursuing. Additionally, Fi lends a degree of closure to ENFP by helping them find suitable resting spots in the exploratory process.

Like ENFP, ENTP use inferior Si, but instead of Te, ENTP use tertiary Fe. The result is, ENTP come across as the warmer, more gregarious type because tradition-oriented Si combines with Fe to make for people who cannot help but ingratiate themselves to their communities. This is even though ENFP are far more aware of their own values and how they came to hold those values than even the most mature ENTP. Similarly, Si in concert with Te means that ENFP come across as far more practical, even logical, than ENTP, even though ENTP's sense of logic cannot be challenged by ENFP. Just as the ENFP can experience far more shades of feelings than an ENTP, so can ENTP spot for more logical nuances than ENFP. These discrepancies between what one sees and what is going on inside are the result of the fact that Ne-dominant types introvert their chief judging function. Si always keeps an eye towards maintaining one's sense of equilibrium and wellbeing, always looking for sensory experiences that bring comfort, not necessarily excitement. Furthermore, Si likes to keep things just the way they have been, looking at change as an often unnecessary and foolish risk. Despite, the exploratory nature of ENFP's dominant function, ENFP are in no way exempt from Si's natural tendencies. One can see this in the way that ENFP often attempt to impose their will on the environment to maximize comfort and minimize risk. Such behavior can take on many forms, from obsessively cleaning, to following stubbornly the same outdated routine, to parsing the language of a speech so that every word's objective meaning meets traditional standards. Perhaps, Si's most important role in ENFP's psychic economy is its ability to constrain Ne's exploration to those things that comport with one's everyday experience of the world.

ENFP are not only adept at finding and exploiting objective possibilities, but have some skill explicating a cohesive underlying meaning to their subjective experience (Ni). This type knows when to rely on gut instinct. However, Ni is difficult even for Ni-dominants to describe, with the best descriptions falling well short of the totality of Ni's role in the psyche—a natural consequence of Ni's highly symbolic nature. It should not be surprising, therefore, that even though ENFP demonstrate some competence using Ni, they do not tend to notice how significant a role Ni plays in their worldview. Ti, on the other hand, is a far more challenging matter. Though ENFP highly value order in the outer world since such order helps them maintain their comfort, this type generally shows disdain for subjective logical systems. "Why does Susan have to make this so complicated? Clearly, there's a simpler way," an ENFP might say. Moreover, relying on formal logical systems goes against ENFP's preferred way of dealing with their inner world, which is through their subjective value systems. These values are distinct from subjective thought, for even though ENFP could readily acknowledge that something they are feeling is illogical, they would also point out that the realization of illogic or impracticality does little to change what they are feeling. Ti, however, stops in its tracks and returns to the starting point when it spots even the slightest degree of logical inconsistency; and at the socially acceptable time, Ti is not above using its counterpart, Fe, to ridicule Fi's pain, which to Ti's eyes, is caused by illogical or inappropriate feelings. Similarly, ENFP's Fi is not above using its counterpart, Te, to point out the absurdity of Ti's hairsplitting ways—hairsplitting that never leads to an understanding of what is most important to oneself. ENFP, however, would do well to remember that one's sense of objective facts, data and figures is necessarily undergirded by a subjective, logical structure; otherwise, such objective considerations would be unassimilable and, consequently, it would be impossible to reach any conclusions whatsoever by means of objective data.

When ENFP's outer and inner personalities are put together, one finds people with an incredible ability to find the best in others and the determination to help others develop to their fullest. Obviously, Ne helps ENFP see people's potential and Fi makes it quite natural to empathize with others since strong Fi users are deeply versed on life's joys and sorrows. Te tells ENFP how to move efficiently between Point A and Point B, providing as many definitions, data sets, rules and maps as necessary to help others reach the stars; and Si helps to make sure that the potentials intuited by ENFP accord with their individual experience of the world. A word people often overlook when considering ENFP's relationship to life is willpower. Most often associated with thinking types, or more dubious still, associated with masculinity, ENFP's will is nonetheless substantial, especially when dealing with mature representatives of this type. This is owing to ENFP's combination of Fi and Te. When something strikes ENFP deeply enough, they will walk to the ends of the earth to make it happen simply because their values are so deeply held. INFP can be moved to action, but because INFP's Te operates as the inferior function, not the tertiary, INFP are not as inclined to make concrete change.

ENFP's perceptions are polarized toward their intuition and, thus, away from their sensation. This polarization is nothing to be ashamed of, for it is the defining characteristic of this type. There is only so much libido available to the psyche, and Ne's oft-excessive use of libido necessarily results in Si being somewhat neglected. This would not be a big problem if ENFP were aware of this tendency but, like every type, ENFP's relationship to their inferior function is lacking to such a degree that they struggle to notice how significant a role the inferior plays in their daily lives. Sure enough, the solution is to honor the inferior function's input because every function is necessary to a truly conscious, even enlightened understanding of life. Each function provides information about reality, whether physical or psychic, that can scarcely afford to be ignored, which is why Jung was so fond of quoting the first words of Plato's *Timaeus*. "One, two, three. But where, my dear Timaeus, is the fourth of those who were yesterday my guests and are to be my entertainers today?" Jung, obviously, interpreted this line psychologically, associating the first three with the dominant, auxiliary and tertiary functions, which are the three functions most people will develop in a lifetime. The fourth, then, represents the inferior function, which is such a challenge to make conscious, that even Socrates, considered the wisest of his time, lost track of it. ENFP are deeply impassioned about asking what if, and because they are comfortable challenging existing norms and beliefs, representatives of this type can be incredible engines for change. ENFP are far less comfortable when forced into a routine or set of traditions that limits this type's exploration—exploration that favors the abstract to the concrete. Though ENFP do not have great body awareness, they highly value comfort and familiarity.

There is far less polarization between ENFP's Fi and Te, on the other hand. This is because Fi, though showing a fair amount of differentiation in ENFP, is not free to steal much of its counterpart's libido (i.e., Fi must submit to ENFP's dominant Ne). It is easy, therefore, to be struck by the power of ENFP's Te, a perception not at all helped by the fact that ENFP's Te is extraverted while its more mature counterpart is introverted. It is this very dynamic that compels ENFP to develop their tertiary function earlier than many of their peers. Though Fi can imply its judgments through Ne, a clear and direct expression of judgment to the outer world requires extraverted judgment. Thus, in order for ENFP's Fi judgments to be expressed with anything close to their actual maturity, or level of consideration, requires facility with the tertiary function. Throw in the fact that ENFP's primary way of structuring the outer world comes through Te, and the need for this accelerated development becomes clear.

Psychology of Se-Ni, Fi-Te Types

ISFP

FI	SE
NI	TE
FE	SI
NE	TI

ISFP are chiefly oriented toward their inner worlds, which are consciously influenced by Fi and, to a lesser extent, Ni. ISFP's unconscious introversion can be understood in terms of Ti and Si.

Because Fi is the dominant function, all ISFP's other functions are necessarily subordinate to Fi's demands.

Fi is associated with personal value judgments, helping the individual to maintain a degree of integrity to oneself, one's ideas of moral or immoral, and enjoyable or unenjoyable. This function, along with Ti, is a primary protector of the individual—protecting the individual from collective and often poorly considered ideas about life and the world. Because no function allows one to get as clear an insight into one's emotional makeup as Fi, ISFP are especially concerned with maintaining an inner sense of harmony and positive feelings, which can only be the result of individual effort. Unlike types who prefer Fe, ISFP are comfortable allowing themselves to feel negative emotions, viewing troublesome feelings equally as important and deserving of examination as positive feelings; and since Fi is oriented towards the subjective factor, it is necessarily oriented to value judgments that apply universally. Thus, ISFP want to know what laws can be applied to valuations of all people, places, things and ideas; and consequently, as societal norms and ideas change about those values, Fi's very nature both guides and resists those changes.

It is impossible to have any conscious awareness of one's values without having some sense, however vague, of meaning. For as a general rule, one does not bother to assign value to things that lack meaning because such things, contents and ideas do not break through into consciousness. This is where Ni becomes important to ISFP. Since this type prioritizes Fi over all other functions, ISFP's mildly undifferentiated use of intuition is imbued with some individuality by means of their superior use of Fi. Where INTJ, who also consciously use Ni and Fi, easily perceive their mental images but have a tougher time determining the images' importance, the situation is reversed for ISFP. The mental images are comparatively vague, but when confronted from within by new, strange or otherwise extreme feeling tones, mature ISFP's Ni goes into overdrive to find the source of the troublesome feelings.

Since Ni is ISFP's most conscious introverted perceiving function, Ni plays a significant part in ISFP's worldview. While ISFP's Ni, which in the tertiary position, lacks the bells and whistles associated with dominant Ni, it nonetheless gives ISFP not only the kind of raw instinct often seen in ESFP, but also allows this type to see what lies beneath the surface. Mature ISFP can also show a profound level of self-awareness, understanding not only their underlying motivations and root values, but also the inner psychic landscape from which those motivations and values arise. When well-developed ISFP couple their depth of self-understanding with their sense of the archetypes—a sense that is generally conscious enough to make ISFP dimly aware of the archetypes, but not conscious enough for ISFP to realize archetypes' inherent multi-sided nature— such ISFP often show a deep understanding of their relationship to the world and their role in it. While such an understanding allows ISFP to live with an artistic richness to life, it does little to prepare ISFP for the inevitable archetypal counter-swing that necessarily results from their primary way of perceiving the outside world: through Se, which, if understood logically, seeks to experience the archetypes by living them as objective realities. One might take the archetype of the hero, for example. One immediately sees an image of invincibility; but, is that all? Is there such a thing as a hero without villains? Clearly not. Do heroes always succeed? Again, the answer is no. It should be clear, then, that all archetypes are multi-sided,[35] even spherical, with the center of the sphere being the archetypal experience and its possibilities *in toto*, and radiating out in all directions from that center radii representing all potential outcomes in concrete form, i.e., only one outcome is possible in physical reality, though the possibilities might seem innumerable at the psychic level.

While most ISFP are aware of their internal physical state, their inner equilibrium or the traditions at work in a situation, ISFP are most comfortable using such knowledge to critique themselves or others. One can even find such criticism at work in the athletic displays so common to this type by observing how ISFP use this largely unconscious awareness of internal physical states to one-up an opponent and place that opponent in an uncomfortable physical position. As a type using dominant feeling, ISFP often show little awareness of the thoughts that must logically be associated with any feeling, and this is especially true when it comes to ISFP's relationship to Ti. ISFP, therefore, are typically uncomfortable with formal logic, deductive analysis and categorization, much preferring to rely on their real-world observations or expert opinion.

ISFP's observable psychology consists most prominently of Se and Te. Ne and Fe's apparent absence in the conscious personality is also a key factor. These components lend the ISFP psychology a kind of gravity and practicality that would otherwise seem to be lacking. Not content simply to think about life, ISFP need to live life and feel a strong urge to experience the new and unique in tangible ways. ISFP dress in a way that stylishly reflects their unique identity and sense of self. Members of this type want their homes to be genuine reflections of who they are. ISFP need to experience the people and things that have brought members of this type positive feelings, seeking not to change those for whom they care, but accepting them as they are—warts and all. ISFP live a life thoroughly in tune with their morals and values, using their strong awareness of the environment and its landscape to avoid situations that have the potential to put this type in a compromising position. Te gives ISFP the power to uphold their values in the outer world and, though ISFP might be a dominant feeling type, the tandem of Te and Se means that ISFP are not afraid of conflict, though they would rather avoid pointless confrontations in the first place. Moreover, mature ISFP have no problem meeting basic Te demands such as arriving to appointments on time, maintaining a clean room or putting furniture together. However, these basic tasks can be a challenge for a young or otherwise poorly developed ISFP, even though ISFP's exploratory nature often makes up for immature Te.

Thoroughly immersed in the here and now, ISFP would love to have everything and everyone they love to be in the here and now, too; but physics makes such a pure archetypal experience impossible, and that is where Te enters the picture, providing ISFP with a sense of the laws that govern tangible reality and society. ISFP's struggle with Te is complicated because Fi constantly strives to uphold the importance of the individual's feelings, ideals and values while Te imposes collective rules, regulations and methods that seem to trample on the individual, at times. This pull between what the individual needs and what society demands of her is a struggle ISFP feel acutely. A struggle that is hindered, not helped, by ISFP's relationship to their inferior function — a relationship characterized by both clumsiness and powerful insights. ISFP often struggle to acclimate to new rules and regulations, changes to familiar systems or large bundles of data. Eventually, mature ISFP find some degree of balance between the individual and society, realizing that all rules and regulations, though laborious, serve to protect the individual in important ways. Laws that make robbery illegal help protect everyone's property; laws regulating the cleanliness of food and water help protect individuals' health; traffic laws help improve safety for drivers, passengers and pedestrians. Though such examples are rather clear cut, they are nevertheless illustrative of this classic struggle between the individual and the collective.

While ISFP are generally attuned to life's comings and goings in an archetypal way, feeling a deep sense of relatedness to the environment, such use of intuition stops with Ni, for ISFP are often disdainful of Ne. Eminently grounded and concrete, ISFP have little patience for the exploration of possibilities, especially possibilities that will never be anything more than just that: possibilities. To ISFP, such exploration is fruitless given the seemingly infinite number of realities deserving exploration. On the other hand, ISFP generally have some skill in Fe matters since ISFP are incredibly aware of how they want to be treated. ISFP, therefore, generally have no problem maintaining a favorable social atmosphere and others tend to connect with the ISFP's generosity of spirit. However, the seemingly inauthentic displays of emotion so characteristic of Fe is anathema to this type. ISFP typically believe that lasting happiness can only come as the result of integrity to themselves and their own values.

When ISFP's inner and outer personalities are put together, one finds that ISFP live a life that is deeply artistic. Fi causes ISFP to receive powerful emotional impulses, feelings so intense that the ISFP can scarcely afford to bottle them up. Se drives members of this type to express their values and ideas in concrete form. With Ni, ISFP are able to explain their creations' meaning—the emotions that inspired their works of art, the symbolism that hints at what lies beneath the surface, the artistic creation's meaning for the future. Te helps ISFP tie their projects together by crafting a plan of action. Just as one finds that the best movies masterfully balance contrasting content—antagonist and protagonist, conflict and reconciliation, climax and resolution—so, too, do many ISFP feel themselves as many people rolled up in a single bag of skin. Members of this type often have a different sense of self depending on the time of the day. When one remembers that this type prefers Se over Ni, the varying sense of self-identity should hardly be surprising since this psychic configuration necessitates that the archetypes be made living realities. The advantage and disadvantage that types who prefer Ni to Se have is that, for them, the archetypes are much more likely to manifest clearly in the conscious mind than one would encounter with ISFP. Jung said, "The psychological rule says that when an inner situation is not made conscious, it happens outside, as fate. That is to say, when the individual remains undivided and does not become conscious of his inner opposite, the world must perforce act out the conflict and be torn into opposing halves."[36] Strong Ni-types are, therefore, much less likely to have to experience the archetypes as a kind of fate emerging from outside of themselves. Nonetheless, ISFP have a good shot of bringing Ni's workings to consciousness because Ni is in no way antagonistic to ISFP's dominant function. Hence, even though ISFP's Ni is mildly undifferentiated, ISFP are not subjected to unconsciously living out the archetypes to the same extent that Se-dominant types might be.

Since Fi is the dominant function, it is liable to steal much of the libido to which Te is entitled. The space between forming a value judgment and applying that value judgment to the outer world can be significant for ISFP, whose live-and-let-live approach to life not only leads them to be mildly suspicious of rules and laws, but averse to applying those rules to others. ISFP are quite strict and regimented about their values, and ISFP find it nearly impossible to act in any way contrary to their personal beliefs and judgments. This type is not nearly as adamant about upholding the rules and laws that ensure not only the continuance of civilized society, but also the protection of individuals. This tension between the individual and society is typical not only of ISFP, but all types who use dominant introverted judgment. ISFP, especially when immature, are prone to resolving this pull between the individual and the collective in favor of themselves. It is not that ISFP are wrong to resolve such tensions in their own favor, for society *always* considers collective needs. However, to the extent that the balance between the individual and society is unconscious, it represents a character flaw deserving of attention. ISFP who have become aware of this inner struggle become beacons for those around them, never hesitating to sound the alarm when the individual is being swallowed by a sea of collective values and thoughts, always reminding the world that if the individual is lost in society, then society itself is lost.

ISFP show much less polarization in their perceptions, for in the auxiliary position, Se does not rob its counterpart, Ni, of as much libido as would be encountered if Se occupied the dominant position. As a result, ISFP's experience of objective reality is deeply informed by their intuitions, and their intuitions are guided by Se's practicality and real-world experience. Mature ISFP are also rather comfortable shifting between big picture, philosophical insights and the nitty-gritty, practical implementation of their ideas. Though they are not as rigorous in their planning as their INTJ counterparts, ISFP are far more comfortable taking real and immediate action, relying more on their ability to adjust on the fly than a plan that has a contingency in place for every obstacle.

INTJ

NI	TE
FI	SE
NE	TI
FE	SI

INTJ are principally oriented toward their inner worlds, which are consciously driven by Ni and, to a lesser extent, Fi. Si and Ti are used unconsciously.

Since Ni is the dominant function, the hero on his journey, all INTJ's other functions are necessarily subordinate to its dictates.

Ni naturally perceives the unfolding of processes over time, perceiving past, present and future all at once. Such ability is the result of Ni's close association with the archetypes, which constitute the psychic substrate, patterns or forms that organize all cognition of human experience.[37] Therefore, Ni-dominant types constantly receive vivid mental images that illustrate these psychic outlines in symbolic form. Not only do these mental images give Ni-dominants a sneak preview of a situation's outcome, they relate the objective situation to the subject in a holistic way. INTJ peer fearlessly below the surface, and they are able to perceive the essence of people, places or things. Members of this type pick up on that special something that makes any object unique, yet at one with all else. This ability to look beyond the obvious most often takes the form of INTJ instantaneously understanding impersonal systems, and how the parts of the system relate to the whole. Since Ni is, by far, the rarest dominant function, Ni-dominants often realize that they are regarded as aloof and a bit strange. Thus, even INTJ unfamiliar with psychological typing have learned that their mental images, while certainly containing objective validity, are expressed in an incredibly subjective, personal manner; and therefore, most INTJ will keep many of their intuitions and hunches to themselves—often holding back this part of themselves from even their closest friends and family.

INTJ do not blindly follow every mental image or hunch, and even if this type were so inclined, there is hardly enough time to follow every intuition to its conclusion. Analogously, Se cannot chase after every novel sensory experience. Thus, in INTJ, every mental image is imbued with a feeling tone that serves to make the INTJ aware, even dimly, of the image's value (i.e., Ni offers a vision or sense of meaning, and Fi steps in to determine how important the vision is.) The stronger the feeling tone Fi assigns to the image, the more INTJ will strive to bring the outer world into conformity with the image or, at least, use the mental image to advance their understanding of the world. Fi, in combination with INTJ's powerful inner vision (Ni) means that INTJ are very strong willed and this type often prevails over difficult circumstances or supposedly unbeatable opposition, not only because of INTJ's superior strategic thinking, but also because INTJ's sense of resolve means that they outlast their competition. Like any Fi type, INTJ can be vengeful, and when they feel they have been wronged, INTJ often administer punishment themselves—punishment that is usually served with a good dose of humiliation. INTJ typically have very high moral standards, but that should not be taken to mean that they have respect for rules and procedures, which

INTJ tend to see as nothing more than recommendations and guidelines for how to maneuver effectively in the real world.

Because Fi is INTJ's top introverted judging function, it plays an outsized role in their worldview. That means while Fi is largely subject to Ni's dictates, Fi has its own needs and a degree of autonomy in helping to meet those needs. People who are familiar with the mountains of literature around psychological types might not expect it, but INTJ are quite sensitive, but because they do not consciously use feeling to operate in the outer world, INTJ are often viewed as cold and emotionally unresponsive. However, dominant Ni allows its user to register the workings of the mind with a level of accuracy rivaling dominant Se's ability to register the details of the outside world. When members of this type couple that sharp insight into themselves with Fi, one finds people who are incredibly self-aware; but instead of completely allowing themselves to feel and work through their negative emotions, INTJ simply take concrete action to eliminate the negative feeling's cause or, else, use Ni to shift to a perspective that is not as painful.

While INTJ often have good command of deductive logic, they are unlikely to use it except to criticize themselves or others, and when such criticism shows its face in INTJ, this type's conclusions can be brutal, yet insightful. In such instances, INTJ can be quite INTP-like in their ability to expose problematic logical assumptions, but it is hard to miss the venom INTJ's Fi injects into such criticism at the same time. INTJ understand the necessity of well-defined terms and logical consistency, but this type tends to look upon overly systematic interpretations with deep skepticism, finding such interpretations arbitrary and inherently incomplete when empirical validation is absent. INTJ, like other dominant intuitives, often show little awareness of their own bodies, which is a natural consequence of INTJ's distant relationship to Si. To the extent that INTJ show any willingness to use Si at all, it is primarily done to find methods and ideas that have worked in the past and to modify those ideas, if needed, to any present challenges.

INTJ's observable personality is most strongly characterized by the combination of Te and Se. Fe and Ne's unconscious use is also a key component. Te and Se help give the INTJ personality a kind of weight that Ni and Fi sometimes fail to confer. Te is INTJ's chief judging function, and it typically gives INTJ the outward appearance of practicality and decisiveness. When Te is combined with Se, it means INTJ want facts and data. This type wants to hear all the expert opinions. When it comes to drawing conclusions, however, INTJ typically believe they are the ones best qualified to do so. They will not easily suffer the reintroduction of ideas or viewpoints that they have already considered and rejected. INTJ rely on clear statements of observable cause and effect to prove their points, not deductive reasoning, which would be rather redundant considering that Ni already lends a degree of perceptual integrity because Ni's perceptions are archetypal. Such integrity is sorely needed, for though INTJ are, perhaps, the type naturally aware of the widest field of data simply owing to the top-down structure of this type's psyche, many details tend to slip by when one is so high in the sky. It would, therefore, be inaccurate to call INTJ, or any other type, the most conscious since many others are intensely aware of the data that, for the INTJ, is a bit out of focus.

Measurable results are what INTJ seek in the outer world, and that leads to INTJ's famous frustration with repeating themselves, stating the obvious or working with those whom are deemed incompetent. While INTJ can be rather demanding of others, those demands in no way measure up to what INTJ expect of themselves. Thus, INTJ generally make for strong leaders, especially when their Fi is well developed. No other type is as good at maintaining a pleasant workplace for their employees by letting unimportant things slide while at the same time using such leniency as rightful justification for maintaining an iron grip on matters of import. While INTJ are comfortable giving direct orders, they would rather explain the context for a given job and what satisfactory results would look like (Se), leaving the method to the employee. Thus, the one demand of an INTJ boss is competence, for without it, the employee could not create the methods needed for success, and instead would constantly intrude on the INTJ for advice that this type will often feel should not be needed. If Fi is poorly developed, however, the INTJ manager would resemble an ENTJ, but with less verbal fluidity. Conscious use of Te and Se results in an incredible economy of communication. Thus, INTJ are happy to state only the most necessary premises and the conclusions that have been drawn, leaving it up to others to fill in the gaps. In this way, INTJ are quite different from their INTP brethren, for INTP generally find it necessary to give most every premise in their arguments, leaving no stone unturned in their explanations. This makes sense when one remembers that INTJ, though they speak through their thinking function, seek an intuitive understanding. INTP, on the other hand, seek a logical understanding even though they speak through their intuitive function.

INTJ are often accused of being unemotional robots. As explained above, that is about as far from the truth as one can get. Te and Se can both come across as cold and unfeeling. Typically, INTJ are aware of their lack of Fe skills and talents, often having been told of the issue many times before reaching adulthood. INTJ's reliance on Te as the chief judging function freezes out Fe in a major way, so members of this type are often unable and somewhat unwilling to meet all but the most basic of Fe's demands. On the other hand, INTJ are more comfortable with Ne than Fe, but generally view Ne's improvisatory style as a bit misguided because Ne is happy to consider possibilities that, to Ni, look implausible or unlikely. When INTJ find themselves in situations that require good improvisatory skills, however, they become painfully aware of Ne's value. For this reason, INTJ rarely perform as well in job interviews or other off-the-cuff remarks as their intelligence and experience might indicate.

When INTJ's inner and outer personalities are put together, one finds someone with incredible planning ability — the best, on average, of all psychological types. Ni allows the user to see the most likely outcomes, allowing the unconscious mind to piece together all the disparate data until Ni brings the unconscious data to awareness. Te lends the skill to develop a clear plan of action to reach the desired result, and the ability to shepherd the right resources at the right times. Fi provides a sense of the result's importance and the fuel to reach the goal, and Se allows INTJ not only to take the concrete steps necessary to realize their vision, but also determine whether the tangible result matches Ni's expectations. INTJ are also lifelong learners, constantly on the lookout for knowledge that would improve not only their own lives, but the entire world. INTJ's learning style could best be characterized as scientific. INTJ use their Ni to theorize based on Se data, and then use their Te to test their theories in search for the truth, which Fi highly values. If one recalls from earlier, conscious awareness of sensations is dependent on feeling and thought; feeling is dependent on thought; and original thoughts are dependent on intuition. With their ordering of the cognitive functions matching this model, INTJ have a natural advantage in consciously fulfilling the individuation process, despite their two biggest hurdles: a natural reliance on collective thought in what is inevitably an individual search for truth and a tendency to want to control each aspect of their lives instead of letting life come to them, as it inevitably would.

INTJ's perceptions are highly polarized toward their intuition and away from their sensing. This should hardly be surprising given that Ni is the dominant function. While this strong polarization allows Ni to function in a highly differentiated and skilled manner, the polarization must also result in occasional incompetent use of Se, which is INTJ's inferior function. Undifferentiated Se is the consequence of Ni using much of the libido to which Se is entitled. As a result, INTJ occasionally struggle to take in volumes of unfamiliar information in a single sitting. With Ni as their go-to function, INTJ easily see how all the parts of a system interact because Ni does not view the system as something outside itself, but as a natural, and archetypal expression of the psyche and its desire to bring the outer world into conformity with one's will and vision. While no type better understands what levers to pull and when, INTJ are not nearly as aggressive in their tendency to make their visions reality as types who use dominant extraverted judgment. Nevertheless, mature INTJ are very demanding, as their inner vision is so pure and clear that INTJ will spare no effort to ensure that the final product matches that vision. Immature representatives of this type, on the contrary, are often paralyzed by a fear that the result will not meet Ni's specifications because the vision's purity is necessarily compromised in its birth into reality.

INTJ, especially when well developed, consistently express judgments that are less polarized between the thinking and feeling functions. That is because Te, though showing a good deal of differentiation in INTJ, is not nearly as potent in the personality as Ni, which means more libido is free to flow to the tertiary function, Fi. Thus, INTJ's judgments are always flavored by implicit value statements, even though the judgments are expressed to the outer world by means of the thinking function. How aware INTJ are of those underlying value judgments depends wholly on INTJ's level of psychological development. This type is more balanced in its decision-making tendencies, however, than types that favor judgment in the dominant position. In less-developed INTJ, there can be a tendency to believe that the greatest flaw in many well-designed systems is the human factor. Incompetent people undermine systems by failing to understand the bigger picture, undertaking inefficient actions and neglecting the real-world consequences of their decisions. Mature INTJ, however, would argue that competent people improve systems like law enforcement or community banking by ascertaining the mission of the system and ensuring that the outcome of each case aligns with those goals, not with an overly rigid interpretation of the laws or policies.

ESFP

SE	FI
TE	NI
SI	FE
TI	NE

ESFP are chiefly oriented to the world of objective reality by way of Se and, to a lesser extent, Te. Fe and Ne are used unconsciously.

Since Se is ESFP's dominant function, all other functions are necessarily subordinate to its demands.

Se allows one to perceive the outer world by means of the five senses. This function concretely deals with life just as it is and bothers little with theoretical considerations. Consequently, ESFP's sense of the world is realistic and down to earth, and because ESFP consciously pair Se with Te, which is also quite practical, ESFP could be considered the most pragmatic type. Strong Se-types have little patience for anyone or anything that does not produce tangible results. Since Se is squarely oriented toward observable reality, ESFP are in tune with their environment and have a fine eye for details. Si-types also have a fine eye for details, but their sense of the details is internal, as Si-types constantly compare the present to the past. Se, on the other hand, is deeply aware of the details in the environment, noting every detail of a Picasso painting, hearing every bit of counterpoint in a Mozart sonata, or taking in every shade of flavor in a favorite dish. ESFP rival even Fe-types at small talk because Se provides ESFP with a steady flow of concrete information to share. Fe's approach depends on establishing a feeling rapport, no matter how superficial. Because Se is an action-packed function, ESFP's instinct is to act immediately when confronted with a problem; and, therefore, ESFP only take the time for deeper reflection as they mature.

At first glance, ESFP and ESTP can seem quite similar because both types use the same dominant function. However, ESFP extravert their thinking function, whereas ESTP extravert their feeling function. In practice, this means that ESFP can seem like a thinking type while ESTP seem like a feeling type — and this is especially true with more mature members of these types. Closer analysis, however, reveals ESFP's true psychology, which sets two cognitive functions ahead of their tertiary Te. ESFP's use of Te, therefore, is not their strong suit, and ESFP only begin to develop any real facility with Te as they mature. That said, even immature use of Te can be seen in ESFP's desire to get immediate results from their actions. Since Te is subordinate to Se in ESFP, one finds that ESFP specialize not so much in long-term or short-term planning, as might be expected in ENTJ and, especially, INTJ, but in determining what rules apply to a given situation and to what extent. "Sure, the traffic light is red, but since no one is here, let's have some fun," an ESFP might say.

In addition to the gamesman-like use of Te is a far more serious use. Te allows one to understand the world in a deeply factual and empirical way. When Te is combined with Se, the function through which people become aware of any concrete information about the outer world, one finds people who are instinctively in tune with the environment. They possess a natural sense of the right tool for the job, improvise on the spot should the right tool not be available and, ultimately, help ensure humanity's survival through an instinctive grasp of the environment and its laws. With Te as the tertiary function, ESFP can rival any type's command of the details because, like Se, Te records details in raw form. However, instead of recording raw sensory data, Te focuses on facts, natural law and society's rules and procedures. With Te as the tertiary function, ESFP make for strong, but somewhat reluctant leaders. They clearly sense the politics at the office and use their own well-developed sense of right and wrong, to maintain an uplifting work environment.

ESFP tend to have some degree of competence using Fe, though its use is not at all preferred by ESFP, who instead use it to criticize themselves and others. Such use would tend to take the form of critical remarks regarding failures to live up to collective values. Even though these remarks tend to affirm society's values, following such criticism back to the source often reveals the cause was a failure to adhere to common-sense rules and procedures. Ne, on the other hand, tends to be far more challenging for ESFP because no other function is as opposed to this type's dominant function as Ne. When Ne's perceptions correspond neatly with Se, one can expect ESFP to show a healthy, but unconscious use of Ne's insights. If, however, Se and Ne perceptions come into conflict, whether real or apparent, expect ESFP to cling even more forcefully to the dominant function's viewpoint instead of taking the time to integrate the supposedly disparate material into the ego's vantage point. Such a reaction is typical of any person who has not yet matured, not just ESFP. Ne functions just as objectively as Se, but instead of dealing with tangible reality, Ne deals with abstractions, like ideas, theories and possibilities. When it comes to possibilities, ESFP find their usefulness tenuous, at best.

"There's no point in worrying about what will happen five years from now," an ESFP might say. "We have enough problems to deal with today."

ESFP's conscious inner world consists of Fi and Ni. Si and Ti are used unconsciously. With Fi as their top introverted function, ESFP are acutely aware of their values, convictions and personal tastes. ESFP decide for themselves what is right or wrong, good or bad, tasteful or tasteless; and more often than not, they live up to their own standards. ESFP use Fi to figure out concrete matters, like what to eat for dinner, where to vacation or what clothes to buy. As ESFP mature and begin to utilize their intuition more, they increasingly contemplate abstract matters like love, faith or even the meaning of life. Because of such contemplation, Fi becomes a moderating force in the ESFP personality, rather than a mere instrument used to determine which sensory experience is most exhilarating. This type is prone to a degree of sentimentality because Fi personalizes one's experiences in a deep way. As a result, ESFP tend to feel a deep bond with their friends and family, a bond not subject to dissolution irrespective of the amount of time or distance separating ESFP from their loved ones; and there is no type more willing to make tangible sacrifices for those near and dear to them than ESFP.

With Ni as the inferior function, ESFP prefer to focus on sensate details, using them to build a vague, but powerful sense of the big picture from the ground up. Ni's workings tend to be a bit mysterious even for those who use Ni as their dominant function. Obviously, this is a much bigger problem for ESFP. With the outlines of their shadow readily observable in their Ni, ESFP are often quick to dismiss their intuition's importance. The problem is, Ni represents a real, yet bewildering, part of reality and, therefore, ESFP cannot afford to ignore Ni's role in their lives. The most precocious members of this type are in tune with their intuition, using it to adapt seamlessly to life's changing circumstances. Much more common, however, are ESFP who are openly distrustful, even disdainful, of intuition; but, no matter how little ESFP listen to their Ni, its significance to their psyche remains. In such cases, ESFP are instinctively compelled to live out the archetypes, which in and of itself, is not the problem since all people, no matter how skillful their use of Ni might be, live out the archetypes. However, what does not become conscious comes to one from outside as fate.[38] Thus, by becoming aware of the archetypes at work in one's psyche, one is spared from meeting many an unnecessary fate. Naturally, that result would ultimately be dependent on an ESFP's capacity for self-reflection.

ESFP are often good at recalling facts, honoring traditions and remembering past sensory experiences in vivid detail. However, Si does not put one in touch with the environment as much as it puts one in touch with one's *sense* of the environment. ESFP, therefore, largely act as if Si is a problem stepchild, even though ESFP would readily acknowledge Si's importance to everyone's psychic economy. ESFP tend to be most aware of their bodies when their live-life-to-the-fullest style has them tired, sore and worn out. Si's inclination to routine and security over open-ended exploration and risk taking is about as far away from ESFP's preferred way of doing things as possible. This reluctance to use Si is the inevitable result of ESFP's preference for using sensation to orient themselves to the outer world, not the inner. Ti, on the other hand, is much more challenging for ESFP, who often do not see the point of overly systematic interpretations of the world.

Therefore, ESFP often find strong Ti-types to be something of an annoyance. ESFP want to deal with their inner world according to their values, and though worldviews must include logical deductions, such logic often remains unconscious in ESFP regardless of validity. For ESFP, the proof of the pudding is in the eating; if an argument has validity, there should be some evidence of that validity in the real world. Lacking such evidence, this type will not hesitate to reject the argument as pointless or incorrect. ESFP, however, are more than willing to change their minds when they find empirical validation—if ESFP feel that they are treated with respect.

ESFP often make talented performers, showing many of the same artistic proclivities observed in ISFP. However, ESFP's urge to act on their artistic impulses is far stronger than one generally sees in ISFP, who are far more selective in their artistic pursuits owing to ISFP's dominant Fi. Where ISFP prefer to make their life a work of art, ESFP are much more likely to make art wherever life takes them, a clear consequence of ESFP's dominant Se, which makes them quite comfortable leaving their options open. However, ESFP have clear ideas about what is worth their time, owing to their auxiliary Fi, and having decided what pursuits they value most, mature ESFP have no problem coming up with concrete steps to change those desires into tangible reality. ESFP tend to discover their place in the world as they attain life experience, and that place is at the forefront of the action. Owing to their combination of Se and Te, ESFP often feel driven to participate in systems that make the world a better place. Unlike their shadow type, ISFJ, ESFP do not work at improving the world by sharing or manipulating communal values. ESFP, instead, take concrete action. "I found a cat on the street, and it is starving," an ESFP might say. "I just had to bring it home." With their combination of Fi and Ni, ESFP do wax philosophical on occasion, focusing on the meaning of life; but owing to the structure of ESFP's mind, a structure most naturally attuned to the concrete aspects of existence and eschewing the abstract in large measure, ESFP will be found living life, not simply thinking about it.

ESFP's perceptions are a strength since Se is ESFP's dominant function. This type's reliance on Se, however, exposes a challenge: a good deal of the libido Ni needs to integrate fully its views into the psyche is stolen by the dominant function. INTJ and INFJ, the types who use dominant Ni, have a similar problem; but since those types cannot function in the world without a healthy amount of sensory awareness, this issue is not as pronounced in them. Indeed, Se-dominant types are the most prone to an imbalance between their dominant and inferior functions because no function is as easy to ignore as Ni. One obviously cannot survive in the world without mindfulness of sensations, neither can people make it too far in society without possessing at least a modicum of cognizance regarding their thoughts and feelings. Intuition, however, is the subtlest of the four factors of consciousness. While it might be tempting to assume that ISTJ and ISFJ are hampered by a similar tendency to ignore their inferior intuition, Si-types use Ne. Because Ne is extraverted, it intrudes upon Si-types' consciousness from the outside with a reality that cannot be denied. ESFP, in some senses, are better off than any other type because ESFP consciousness is structured so that the most concrete aspects of reality are clearest. That means that so many of the details and practicalities that elude other types are rarely unnoticed by ESFP. On the other hand, it also means that the more abstract nuances of reality, which come from intuition and thinking are sometimes overlooked. Thus, by giving more attention to meaning, possibilities or long-term consequences, ESFP expand their conscious awareness and decrease the degree of polarization between their dominant and inferior functions.

ESFP typically show far less polarization between their auxiliary Fi and tertiary Te. Se prevents Fi from robbing the libido Te needs to reach consciousness. This close connection between Fi and Te means that ESFP are highly concerned with fairness, which is a central issue for all Fi-Te types. Immature ESFP tend to be most concerned with what is fair *to them* and actively structure the outer world in ways designed to meet that expectation. Mature ESFP, on the contrary, think about fairness from a more cosmopolitan perspective and readily consider the impact of their own actions on others. ESFP will show far less volatility in their judgments than their ISFP cousins, for whom the Fi-Te judgment dichotomy is the animating psychological force. An easy way to distinguish between the two types is ESFP's quick movement between forming a value judgment and applying it to the outer world — movement that is much more deliberate and cautious in ISFP.

ENTJ

TE	NI
SE	FI
TI	NE
SI	FE

ENTJ are primarily oriented to the outer world of objective reality through Te and, to a lesser extent, Se. Fe and Ne are used unconsciously.

Since Te is ENTJ's dominant function, all other functions are necessarily subject to its dictates, demands and point of view.

Te brings order to the world, focusing chiefly on impersonal processes, data and systems, and dealing with persons only insofar as those persons are parts of the systems or data. No other function is as important to the drafting, implementation and enforcement of rules, policies and regulations as Te because it instinctively understands how cause leads to effect in objective, impersonal systems. Thus, even when ENTJ lack total command of deductive reasoning, they nonetheless make decisions that help them reach their goals far more often than not. This sharp decisiveness is distinctive of Te and, therefore, one of the principal characteristics of ENTJ, who often find themselves taking the lead in their groups — not by any effort to force themselves into the lead role, but by sheer force of personality. Just as INTP, who lead with Ti, suppress emotions to gain a clear image of the logic and structure underlying the world, ENTJ do the same. Instead of suppressing group values, however, it is ENTJ's own values that are lost in the shuffle.

While such suppression imbues ENTJ and ESTJ, who also use dominant Te, with the archetypal image of the manager or executive, the suppression causes all sorts of problems because ENTJ sometimes forget to attend to the other part of the judgment process: feeling.

Since ENTJ and ESTJ share the same dominant function, it can be hard to tell the two types apart. This problem is in no way helped by the fact that both types use the perception dichotomy in the auxiliary and tertiary positions. In their outer presentations, ENTJ often seem more practical than ESTJ, even though SJ types are known for their practicality. Remember, appearances can be deceiving. ENTJ, unlike ESTJ, extravert their sensation. Hence, ENTJ's communications and decisions tend to bear a clear resemblance to observable reality, with this type often judging the most complex and intricate matters as if the matters were simple affairs. Such an approach means that ENTJ are quickly able to make decisions that other types would struggle to resolve. On the other hand, tertiary Se can lead immature ENTJ to make decisions in need of constant revision.

With Se in the tertiary position, ENTJ are much more likely to take concrete action than INTJ, who use Se in the inferior position. For that reason, ENTJ are often confused for ESTP, whose take-no-prisoners approach to life often causes people to mistake the two types. Compared to most other types, ENTJ and INTJ are strong leaders and planners, but there are some clear distinctions between their styles. INTJ leadership is heavily centered around superior planning, securing buy-in from the appropriate parties and, when mature, constantly weighing the importance of every step, person and goal in any plan. ENTJ, on the other hand, are not nearly as fixated on planning as INTJ, though most ENTJ plans will be far more thorough than other types' plans. ENTJ are focused to a greater degree on taking concrete actions to reach their goals; so instead of expending energy planning every detail, when those details are likely to change, ENTJ get the ball rolling and adjust as necessary. ENTJ are comfortable with that approach because, unlike INTJ, taking immediate action with little or no time to plan comes naturally. ENTJ, however, have a much harder time ascertaining the importance of the steps in their plans. ENTJ are, therefore, at a disadvantage to INTJ in such matters. INTJ are often able to determine immediately how important a step is to reach their goal because INTJ demonstrate more competence with Fi, which for ENTJ, is sometimes no more than a footnote to their plans.

As characteristic of the anti-auxiliary function, ENTJ primarily use Ne to criticize themselves or others, which could take the form of exploring real-world factors indicative of incompetence or possible reasons for an adverse outcome. Ne usage could take on an even darker tone, for ENTJ sometimes use Ne to demonstrate how a given result means one is a failure in the eyes of the world. In times of stress, ENTJ might envision many ways in which things could go wrong, and this type shares those opinions without hesitation. Fe, on the other hand, is more challenging for ENTJ since it is the function most opposed to ENTJ's preferred mode of operation: through Te. ENTJ are not naturally in tune with their own feelings, values and emotions, much less those of society. Because ENTJ are so practical, they will often tolerate Fe usage since no other function is more effective at motivating others to rise to the occasion. However, ENTJ are often unaware that they have run afoul of a collective value until others have taken the time to point out the issue.

ENTJ's conscious introversion consists of Ni and, to a much lesser extent, Fi; their unconscious introversion of Ti and Si. With Ni as the lead introverted function, ENTJ are quite adept at getting a look behind the big picture. The people with whom ENTJ interact often feel as if ENTJ can see right into others' souls. Though ENTJ might not agree that they have this kind of x-ray vision into other people's natures, ENTJ do easily find gaps in processes or systems, allowing their auxiliary Ni to find the sources of any discrepancies between ENTJ's vision of success and the empirical results. While ENTJ's Ni typically does not show the same level of differentiation that one would encounter in INTJ and INFJ, ENTJ's Ni nonetheless acts as a lighted city upon a hill, serving as a beacon for where this type's projects and agendas must go. ENTJ do receive mental images from time to time, but owing to Te's demand for practicality, these mental images are rarely the decisive factor for ENTJ. Their intuition generally feels like a hunch that they must act on, or if a situation requires immediate action, ENTJ's intuition functions as a kind of gut instinct, much like one sees in SP types. Far more than SP types, however, ENTJ consciously use Ni to understand the world; as a result, ENTJ's instinct does not apply as much to the physical world as it does the mental world. "I just know that moving the company to a new site is the right move, even though the facts say the impact on the bottom line will be minimal," an ENTJ might say. "The outdoor recreation area at the new site will boost employee happiness and, thus, output. I know it's impossible to estimate the quantitative results of qualitative change, but I also know it is the right move."

As pointed out before, ENTJ are generally out of touch with their Fi and, consequently, ENTJ are prone to going all out for each portion of their projects, even portions that do little to alter the bottom line in the end. Similarly, ENTJ will often correct their subordinates brutally, even when the issue being corrected is insignificant to ENTJ's goals. One then finds ENTJ isolated from those under their direction and, as a result, ENTJ must rely on greater and greater brutality to advance their agendas. ENTJ hold strong values; otherwise, they would not get so worked up over minor issues. It is simply that because ENTJ's Fi shows little to no differentiation, so too are ENTJ's values poorly differentiated. Thus, everything either seems to have similar importance, or else, small issues are blown out of proportion and critical issues made into a trifle. Even undifferentiated Fi, however, has a keen sense of one universal value: fairness. Thus, ENTJ's sometimes brutal approach is matched by an equal willingness to interpret the rules the same way no matter who is involved.

ENTJ are often able to understand the deductive logic underlying their decisions, and if compelled to do so, ENTJ can explain their beliefs in a coherent way. However, this type has little patience for relying on such principles to make decisions because those principles are prone to leaving out key real-world facts critical to successful implementation. For example, the best blueprints for a house mean little if the blueprints fail to account for key details like the fact that the house will be built on a slope of 30 degrees. Thus, while types with strong Ti are quick to attack Te's seeming ignorance of deductive logic's principles, ENTJ are ready to answer by simply letting the results speak for themselves. Si, on the other hand, is a much more sensitive matter for ENTJ because nothing bothers them more than being forced to stick to past methods for achieving success when, to ENTJ, it is so obvious that a new idea might work better.

Combine such a view with ENTJ's need to act immediately on their impulses, and one quickly realizes that ENTJ could struggle with types who use Si consciously. Moreover, ENTJ tend to be profoundly out of touch with their own bodies, often engaging in a way of life that results in excessive stress and fatigue. At the same time, Si is not only something ENTJ loathe, but also something to which ENTJ aspire. ENTJ are very concerned with looking the part, working in jobs that have traditionally garnered respect from others and dressing inappropriately stylish ways. While ENTJ express such tendencies via Se, it is hard to miss Si's influence on ENTJ's point of view.

When ENTJ's inner psychology is combined with their outer, one finds the executive par excellence. ENTJ's ability to drive efficiently toward a goal, envision via intuition how the parts relate to the whole, use Se to adapt to unforeseen circumstances and implement plans in a fair way (Fi) are characteristics of visionary leaders. As such, ENTJ are rarely content simply holding the fort and, instead, want to take their team or project in a new or improved direction. ENTJ's combination of Te and Se means that ENTJ are not satisfied with merely thinking about how to move from Point A to Point B, they want to get the job done today. ENTJ want measurable results for all their efforts, and it is best for those who are under this type's direction not to substitute talk for action. ENTJ are not readily fooled about such matters and this type is generally undeterred from challenging firmly and directly anyone's objective contributions to the team or the bottom line. ENTJ tend either to be fully engaged with every aspect of the big picture, sparing no effort in making certain every important detail is fully in place or, otherwise, ENTJ are absolutely disengaged, which is common when ENTJ feel that their ideas are not valued or respected. At such times, ENTJ can show a level of bitterness or even sorrow that is ostensibly more likely to be seen in a feeling type.

With Te as the dominant function, much of the libido to which Fi is entitled is siphoned off. Hence, there is a high degree of polarization in the ENTJ judgment process, with Te showing a good deal of differentiation and Fi showing virtually none. The aforementioned emotional outbursts should hardly shock anyone since Fi is an aspect of humanity's psychic reality that will not be suppressed out of existence. If Beebe's model is correct, Fi, being ENTJ's inferior function, is the carrier of the anima/animus complex. In the case of the anima, Jung said, "This feminine aspect is essentially a certain kind of inferior relatedness to the surroundings, and particularly to women, which is kept carefully concealed from others as well as from oneself."[39] Naturally, one could expect a similar kind of relatedness in the case of the animus. Though ENTJ would be better served by acknowledging their anima/animus, the next best thing is to embrace such emotional outbursts. Though such outbursts can be embarrassing, they serve to integrate unconscious contents because, in addition to consisting of an inferior relatedness, the anima/animus form the bridge from the inferior function, through the shadow and to the superordinate aspect of human psychology that Jung called Self. As such, the anima/animus complex serves to mediate between shadow and the deepest parts of the unconscious mind and, therefore, any efforts ENTJ make towards allowing Fi its proper place in their lives will surely pay off, not only in improved relationships, but also in more effective leadership.

Generally, ENTJ show far less polarization between their auxiliary Ni and tertiary Se. With Te as the dominant function,

Ni is prevented from robbing Se of the libido it needs to reach consciousness. With such a configuration, no type is more comfortable moving from the big picture to the details as ENTJ; and despite the clear role Te plays in ENTJ's success, this easy flow between Ni and Se is also a clear factor since the perceptions from these two functions gives ENTJ's Te the data it needs to form sound judgments. With Se in the tertiary position, and inferior Fi sometimes feeling embittered, ENTJ are not at all above relying on status symbols like luxury cars and expensive suits to make themselves feel a sense of self-value that is sometimes lacking. The easy flow between Ni and Se, however, means that ENTJ usually show far more restraint in those matters than one would expect in Se-dominant types, with ENTJ sometimes showing a disdain for status symbols more in line with INTJ, who often view such symbols as silly — though INTJ are willing to play the game if it will lead to long-term success. With auxiliary Ni, ENTJ can be highly theoretical, but with Se right next door, ENTJ not only expect theories to show tangible results, this type also tends to trust theories that have emerged from empirical observation. That tendency, however, often recedes as ENTJ mature and grow even more comfortable with their intuition.

In Conclusion

The dichotomous nature of the psyche should now be clear. People are not conscious or unconscious, introverted or extraverted, perceivers or judgers; neither is any person a thinker or feeler, an intuitive or sensor. While Myers and Briggs's work has simplified Jung's original insights, it has led to some confusion—even in the most esteemed circles. Namely, people are led to believe that they are only one side of the coin. All people embody the totality of these dichotomies, however. Just as a magnet demands two poles, so too, does every act of perception and judgment.

Many criticize the MBTI®[40] assessment, sometimes for valid reasons. The test not only forces people to choose one side of each dichotomy, the accuracy of the results is dependent on the self-awareness of the test-takers—a most unscientific variable. Despite those valid criticisms, it seems most impossible to conceive of any manner of judgment that is not thought or feeling at its essence, and it is equally implausible that any method of perception shall be found that is not intuition or sensation at its core. Moreover, both introversion and extraversion are necessary to the existence of any sentient being.

The criticisms that go beyond the inherent difficulties in scientifically validating type, therefore, tend to show poor understanding not only of Jung's theoretical framework, but also MBTI's application of his theory. The most frequent criticism is that MBTI claims that one is either an extravert or an introvert, which in consideration of the previous exploration seems almost self-refuting. Most disagreements with typology are along those lines. "I tested as an ESFP in January, but now the test says I'm an INTJ. Clearly, I'm a thinker and feeler, so this test must be bogus."

To be fair, those are criticisms that the very simplicity of MBTI's four-letter codes seems to welcome. If the people who levied such criticism understood the type codes with any depth, however, they surely would have withheld those objections. The type codes only describe the nature of the two most conscious cognitive functions, not the totality of the psychology.

Moreover, much of the criticism is anathema to the scientific spirit—a spirit centered around the pursuit of knowledge, wherever it might lead. Science is only one way of obtaining knowledge. It, therefore, seems most unreasonable to reject MBTI personality types *and* the underlying theory on the basis that the test is prone to human error, or on the basis that there is no physical proof of the cognitive functions. Indeed, if one accepts the seemingly inevitable conclusion that thought, feeling, intuition, sensation, introversion and extraversion are the primary instruments of the psyche, the cognitive functions are an almost necessary implication.

Long before the scientific revolution, many great minds were possessed by tremendous insight into the nature of the psyche. Even a cursory glance through the annals of ancient philosophy make clear that the first philosophers were also the first psychologists. In other cases, psychological insights were largely unconscious and, consequently, the psyche's power was projected onto the environment instead of remaining where it is most potent: with the subject.

Therefore, the next book in this series will look at what philosophers have written about the psychology of personality, and it will analyze many systems of thought that attempted to codify, though vaguely, the roles of thought, feeling, sensation and intuition in the mind's operations.

If you have enjoyed this book, please leave a review. To contact the author for engagements, please write to us at TimelyTypes@TetragramPress.com.

Bibliography

Arraj, J. (2017, May 19). *Jungian Analyst Talks About Psychological Types: A Visit with John Beebe.* Retrieved from Inner Explorations: http://www.innerexplorations.com/catpsy/a.htm

Beebe, J. (2008). *Evolving the Eight-function Model.* Retrieved from C.G. Jung Society of Atlanta: http://www.jungatlanta.com/articles/winter08-evolving-the-eight-function-model.pdf

Heffner, C. L. (2017, 3 24). *Freud's Structural and Topographical Model.* Retrieved from All Psych: https://allpsych.com/psychology101/ego/

Id, Ego and Super-ego. (2017, 2 24). Retrieved from Wikipedia: https://en.wikipedia.org/wiki/Id,_ego_and_super-ego

Jung, C. G. (1953). *Two Essays in Analytical Psychology.* Princeton: Princeton University Press.

Jung, C. G. (1958). *Psychology and Religion: West and East.* New York: Pantheon Books, Inc.

Jung, C. G. (1959). *Aion Researches into the Phenomenology of the Self.* Princeton: Princeton University Press.

Jung, C. G. (1959). *The Archetypes and the Collective Unconscious.* Princeton: Princeton University Press.

Jung, C. G. (1963). *Mysterium Coniunctionis.* Princeton: Princeton University Press.

Jung, C. G. (1964). Approaching the Unconscious. In *Man and His Symbols*. Dell Publishing.

Jung, C. G. (1967). *Alchemical Studies*. Princeton: Princeton University Press.

Jung, C. G. (1969). *Structure and Dynamics of the Psyche*. Princeton: Princeton University Press.

Jung, C. G. (1971). *Psychological Types*. Princeton: Princeton University Press.

Jung, C. G. (1990). *The Undiscovered Self*. Princeton: Princeton University Press.

Jung, C. G., & Harris, J. R. (2016). *The Quotable Jung*. Princeton: Princeton University Press.

Keirsey, D. (1998). *Please Understand Me II*. Del Mar: Prometheus Nemesis Book Company.

Machiavelli, N. (2007). *The Prince*. New York: Watkins Publishing Limited.

Myers, I. B., & Myers, P. B. (1995). *Gifts Differing*. Mountain View: CPP, Inc.

Plato. (2007). *Six Great Dialogues*. Mineola: Dover Publications, Inc.

Notes

1. Plato, 2007, pp. 4-5

2. Jung, Psychological Types, 1971, p. 5

3. Jung, The Undiscovered Self, 1990, p. 25

4. We understand the ego as the complex factor to which all conscious contents are related. It forms, as it were, the centre of the field of consciousness; and, in so far as this comprises the empirical personality, the ego is the subject of all personal acts of consciousness. The relation of a psychic content to the ego forms the criterion of its consciousness, for no content can be conscious unless it is represented to a subject. (Jung, Aion Researches into the Phenomenology of the Self, 1959, p. 3)

5. The personal unconscious is personified by the shadow. (Jung, Mysterium Coniunctionis, 1963, p. 106)

6. Jung, Psychological Types, 1971, p. 333

7. Myers & Myers, 1995, p. 13

8. Jung, Two Essays in Analytical Psychology, 1953, p. 53

9. The self, as a symbol of wholeness, is a coincidentia oppositorum [coming together of opposites], and therefore contains light and dark simultaneously. (Jung & Harris, The Quotable Jung, 2016, p. 51)

10. The "squaring of the circle" is one of the many archetypal motifs which form the basic patterns of our dreams and

fantasies. But it is distinguished by the fact that it is one of the most important of them from the functional point of view. Indeed, it could even be called the *archetype of wholeness*. Because of this significance, the "quaternity of the One" is the schema for all images of God as depicted in the visions of Ezekiel, Daniel and Enoch, and as the representation of Horus with his four sons also shows. (Jung, The Archetypes and the Collective Unconscious, 1959, p. 388)

11. Jung, Psychological Types, 1971, pp. 333-334

12. Jung, Psychological Types, 1971, p. 338

13. Jung, The Archetypes and the Collective Unconscious, 1959, p. 48

14. Jung, Psychological Types, 1971, pp. 373-374

15. Jung, Psychological Types, 1971, p. 378

16. By ego I understand a complex of ideas which constitutes the centre of my field of consciousness and appears to possess a high degree of continuity and identity. Hence I also speak of an ego-complex. The ego-complex is as much a content as a condition of consciousness, for a psychic element is conscious to me only in so far as it is related to my ego-complex. But inasmuch as the ego is only the centre of my field of consciousness, it is not identical with the totality of my psyche, being merely one complex among other complexes. I therefore distinguish between the ego and the self, since the ego is only the subject of my consciousness, while the self is the subject of my total psyche, which also includes the unconscious. In this sense the self would be an ideal entity which embraces the ego. (Jung, Psychological Types, 1971, p. 425)

17. The self is by definition the totality of all psychic facts and contents. It consists on one side of our ego consciousness

that is included in the unconscious like a smaller circle in a greater one. So the self is not only an unconscious fact, but also a conscious fact: the ego is the visibility of the self. Of course, in the ego the self only becomes dimly visible, but you get under favourable conditions a fair idea of it through the ego—not a very true picture, yet it is an attempt. . . . The self consists, then, of the most recent acquisitions of the ego consciousness and on the other side, of the archaic material. The self is a fact of nature and always appears as such in immediate experiences, in dreams and visions, and so on; it is the spirit in the stone, the great secret which has to be worked out, to be extracted from nature, because it is buried in nature herself. It is also most dangerous, just as dangerous as an archetypal invasion because it contains *all* the archetypes: one could say an archetypal experience was the experience of the self. It is like a personification of nature and of anything that can be experienced in nature, including what we call God. (Jung & Harris, The Quotable Jung, 2016, pp. 49-50)

18. In the introverted attitude sensation is based predominantly on the subjective component of perception. What I mean by this is best illustrated by works of art which reproduce external objects. If, for instance, several painters were to paint the same landscape, each trying to reproduce it faithfully, each painting will be different from the others, not merely because of differences in ability, but chiefly because of different ways of seeing; indeed, in some of the paintings there will be a distinct psychic difference in mood and the treatment of colour and form. These qualities betray the influence of the subjective factor. (Jung, Psychological Types, 1971, pp. 393-394)

19. Keirsey, 1998, p. 38

20. Jung, Psychological Types, 1971, pp. 442-443

21. Myers & Myers, 1995

22. Jung, Psychological Types, 1971, pp. 378-380

23. Myers & Myers, 1995, p. 75

24. Jung, Psychological Types, 1971, p. 396

25. Heffner, 2017

26. Id, Ego and Super-ego, 2017

27. Arraj, 2017

28. Beebe, 2008

29. Modern psychology knows that the personal unconscious is only the top layer, resting on a foundation of a wholly different nature which we call the collective unconscious. The reason for this designation is the circumstance that, unlike, the personal unconscious and its purely personal contents, the images in the deeper unconscious have a distinctly mythological character. That is to say, in form and content they coincide with those widespread primordial ideas which underlie the myths. They are no longer of a personal but of a purely supra-personal nature and are therefore common to all men. For this reason they are to be found in the myths and legends of all people and all times, as well as in individuals who have not the slightest knowledge of mythology. (Jung & Harris, The Quotable Jung, 2016, pp. 12-13)

30. At that time it seemed to me a matter of no importance that *The Secret of the Golden Flower* is not only a Taoist text concerned with Chinese yoga, but is also an alchemical treatise. A deeper study of the Latin treatises has taught me better and has shown me that the alchemical character of the text is of prime significance, though I shall not go into this point more closely here. I would only like to emphasize that it was the text

of the Golden Flower that first put me on the right track. For in medieval alchemy we have the long-sought connecting link between Gnosis and the processes of the collective unconscious that can be observed in modern man. (Jung, Alchemical Studies, 1967, p. 4)

31. Jung, Psychological Types, 1971, p. 395

32. Jung, Alchemical Studies, 1967, p. 52

33. Introverted intuition apprehends the images arising from the *a priori* inherited foundations of the unconscious. These archetypes, whose innermost nature is inaccessible to experience, are the precipitate of the psychic functioning of the whole ancestral line; the accumulated experiences of organic life in general, a million times repeated, and condensed into types. In these archetypes, therefore, all experiences are represented which have happened on this planet since primeval times. The more frequent and the more intense they were, the more clearly focussed they become in the archetype. The archetype would thus be, to borrow from Kant, the noumenon of the image which intuition perceives and, in perceiving, creates. (Jung, Psychological Types, 1971, pp. 400-401)

34. Machiavelli, 2007, p. 124

35. Jung, The Archetypes and the Collective Unconscious, 1959, p. 226

36. Jung, Aion Researches into the Phenomenology of the Self, 1959, p. 71

37. Archetypes are, by definition, factors and motifs that arrange the psychic elements into certain images, characterized as archetypal, but in such a way that they can be recognized only from the effects they produce. They exist preconsciously, and presumably they form the structural dominants of the

psyche in general. They may be compared to the invisible presence of the crystal lattice in a saturated solution. As *a priori* conditioning factors they represent a special, psychological instance of the biological "pattern of behavior," which gives all living organisms their specific qualities. Just as the manifestations of this biological ground plan may change in the course of development, so also can those of the archetype. Empirically considered, however, the archetype did not ever come into existence as a phenomenon of organic life, but entered into the picture with life itself. (Jung & Harris, The Quotable Jung, 2016, pp. 16-17)

38. Jung, Aion Researches into the Phenomenology of the Self, 1959, p. 71

39. Jung, Approaching the Unconscious, 1964, p. 17

40. Myers-Briggs Type Indicator, Myers-Briggs, MBTI and MBTI Logo *are trademarks or registered trademarks of the MBTI® Trust, Inc., in the United States and other countries.*

www.ingramcontent.com/pod-product-compliance
Lightning Source LLC
Chambersburg PA
CBHW031504270326
41930CB00006B/237